Contents

Dedicated to
Fred Moegenburg

Inspired by my son,
Beau,
and my daughter,
Sherri Jo

Foreword

Women have been underestimated since time
began. There are qualities in most women that
have never been exercised. Because of vanity, lack
of wanting to try, fear of failure, or embarrassment,
many have fallen into a dependency on others. By
using everything that God has given you and being
honest, you can be sure that a very full life is in
your future.

Words I live by: Always remember there are more
than eight hours in a day. Get another job when
needed to pay your bills. Live within your means.
When in doubt, use common sense and your first
instinct to make decisions.

J. H.

Entrepreneur and Entertainer

There was no such thing as an allowance in our family, and both my parents worked really hard. I guess that explains why an aggressive business gene surfaced in me at a very early age. I never wanted to be home because I would rather be out earning spending money.

I always found a way.

Starting when I was just six years old, I made loop potholders and sold them for 50 cents a pair. There were taverns on just about every corner in our neighborhood and that's where I sold the most. Back then no one got too excited about a little kid going into an establishment that sold food and alcohol and was full of cigarette smoke. I took a quarter from each sale and bought loops to make more potholders.

Later I started selling tins of Cloverine Salve for a dollar. I was proud to be an agent for the Wilson Chemical Company and their salve, which has been on the market since 1895. I made sure that all neighbors, relatives, business owners and just about anybody that crossed my path had their tin of salve. The customers could get a free glossy 9-by-11 picture with each tin. The best part was shopping in their catalog with the points I earned on my sales. The first item I earned was a Brownie camera. Once I had that camera, it was the end of my career with Cloverine Slave.

One year, when I was just a Brownie, I sold more than

6

100 boxes of Girl Scout cookies door-to-door, all on my own. I earned a pin that made me very proud.

But all this was just the beginning. Little did I know that salesmanship was to be my future. This is my story.

I was born at home, in Milwaukee, Wisconsin, in 1944, the second of four children. By 1955, Milwaukee was a big city of about 700,000 people. There were little neighborhoods all throughout the city.

We lived on Farwell Avenue, and I went to Cass Street School from kindergarten until sixth grade. School, overall, was okay. One teacher named Miss Krize was my favorite.

Where kids walked to school, I ran. Even in first grade, I was pretty hardheaded. One day the teacher yanked my pigtails to get my attention as she walked by. This ticked me off. The next time she walked by my desk, she caught me doodling and yanked my hair. I grabbed her arm and bit her wrist and didn't let go. Of course, I got sent to the principal's office, then punished and suspended. I couldn't go out for recess for a week. Naturally, that was nothing compared to what was waiting for me when I got home.

We lived in a one-bedroom apartment in a typical four-unit building. My parents converted one part of the attic into another room, which they rented to boarders. My older brother slept here until he joined the service. My sister and I slept on bunk beds in the same room as my mother and dad. The basement had four separate units, so the tenants each had their own storage, laundry room, coal furnace and coal bin.

Nobody in our neighborhood was rolling in dough, but looking back, now I see why. During World War II, sugar, chocolate, butter, meat, nylons, clothes, shoes, towels and bedding were either rationed or impossible to get. Between 1942 and 1946, no cars were manufactured in the U.S. and you could buy only three or four gallons of gas a week. After the war ended and factories shifted from the military to consumer production, my dad always had a nice car

My mother enjoying her new kitchen.

and money to stop in bars for drinks with his friends after work. People were happy to shop and finally have something to buy.

Dad was from a Polish family from Hatley, Wisconsin, a small village of 300 souls about 180 miles from Milwaukee. His family of 11 were hard-working farm men. Farm work was tough and there was lots of it. My mother wasn't going to be lured into doing anything like that. She knew the more she did, the more my dad would expect her to do.

My mother, Rose, was a housewife. There were 10 in her family of Croatian Catholics. She was from Ontonagon, Michigan, on Lake Superior in the Upper Peninsula, and was born in 1921. My mom never had any hobbies. She didn't want to sew, so she bought all our clothes. Sometimes she'd darn a sock or two, but that's all.

She didn't garden or bake either. I remember lots of oatmeal, Campbell's soup, bologna sandwiches, and just about everything made with noodles, mostly elbow macaroni. Macaroni and cheese, macaroni and hamburger, macaroni salad. No salads, mostly canned vegetables. My sister and brother thought mom was a really good cook, but the only thing she made from scratch was maybe turkey, some cabbage rolls and beef roast. She also made chili with noodles from scratch and also vegetable soup.

Mom wouldn't drive, or even try to, because then she'd have to drive us. She had our father drive us when it was needed. Only once can I can remember when she took me somewhere on a bus.

Being from a blue collar Catholic family on the East Side, there was very little money around. Back then, my dad, as most dads, was against women working outside the home. The idea was that the wife would only get the money the husband gave to her. But after my mother realized she would never get any money other than for groceries, she'd take side jobs, such as ironing or cleaning, while my dad was working a second shift. She'd be able to slide a couple of jobs in for neighbors too, without his ever finding out.

I was about eight when I had to have glasses. My dad didn't want to pay for them, but of course he did. One day I made the mistake of forgetting them on the dresser at home and got a spanking. I never ever forgot them again.

And then there was my little sister, Susie (nicknamed Baby until brother John came along). She was a lot younger than me, so I was the one giving the orders when we did dishes. I always wanted to wipe and told her to wash, which made a bigger mess and took more time to clean up.

One time she resisted me and stood her ground. As I moved toward her, she cuffed her foot around my leg and gave me a push. Down I went, flat on my back, with her foot on my chest. She told ME to wash the dishes. Looked like those karate lessons were paying off.

At age 10, I babysat for seven children. Their mother, Marie Fuller, managed a pizza parlor owned by Sam DeQuardo. Sam realized how responsible I was and had

Marie give me jobs making things like spaghetti sauces and meatballs, all from scratch. My pay was 60 cents an hour. As time passed, I pretty much made ALL the supplies. Sam expanded his pizza places throughout the city and I supplied all of them. His chain predated Shakey's and Pizza Hut. He had a knack for making money. For example, he put in a bid to sell mini-pizzas at the Milwaukee Braves stadium. We would make more than 1,000 pizzas and sell them for a $1.00 each at the home games all summer. After many years, I made $1.60 an hour plus all the pizza I wanted for my friends.

My dad had been a machinist for International Harvester for 21 years when he bought a modest-aged house a few blocks away on Warren Avenue. I was twelve. My mother was very pleased with the new kitchen cabinets that were added after we moved in.

Also when I was twelve, my mother had a baby boy. She named him John. My mother wasn't too happy about this new addition to the family. There was quite an age difference between my little sister and our new baby, John. He was almost like my own baby, and I took him everywhere I could as he got older. John made me want to have kids of my own someday.

Sunday mornings, we kids were sent off to church, then later Mom and her girlfriend went after we got back home. Those were the days when girls always wore dresses to church and school, even in the winter and deep snow. For church I also had a little hat or scarf and gloves. Also, I always had to carry a freshly ironed handkerchief and a dollar for the collection basket.

One day at catechism after church, we had to do a drawing depicting what we'd learned from the Epistles. I drew *The Angels Being Driven Out of Heaven*. I drew them in a gangster's jalopy, a roadster full of them. I thought I did a pretty good job on it, but I got my hand smacked with a ruler by the nun.

Looking back, I remember the days the ice man came

in his big truck. All the neighborhood kids would meet the truck and the driver would chip off slivers of crystal clear ice for all of us to enjoy. After we all got some, he would take his set of huge tongs, grip a block of ice over his shoulder and deliver it to my house. We had our icebox in the hallway, easy to get to without making a mess.

When we got our new refrigerator, it went in the kitchen. My mother always bought margarine because it was less expensive than butter. I got the job of adding the packet of coloring that came with it, mixing it in to make the margarine yellow.

My folks took in boarders to make ends meet. They were fed first. We kids (my older brother, Bob, and younger sister, Susie), along with the other kids that might be there visiting from time to time, ate at a separate table. Kids had no business listening to adult conversations or butting in.

My father worked the second shift, 3 p.m. until midnight, with weekends off. On weekends, he would salvage all the scrap wood and lumber from buildings torn down in the city's redevelopment sites. This would become a job for my sister and me to clean up. We pulled out all the nails and straightened any crooked nails for him to use. We stacked the good lumber for reuse and piled the junk lumber for later use as fire starter with the coal. It would also be used in the pot-bellied stove in the laundry room, our back-up heat.

Dad always kept busy, rarely missing even one day of work, but he took time for barhopping. It was a way of life in the neighborhood. It wasn't unusual for the Catholic priest to stop in at the tavern across the street from church for a beer after the last Mass on Sunday. Some people said he was looking for donations. The bar customers obliged while buying the priest a beer or two. I suppose his theory was, "I can't get them to come to Mass, so I'll take the Mass over to them."

My mother cleaned at a shop called Nancy White

Antiques, owned by a lady named Anita. It was down the street, about two blocks from our house. I walked Anita's dog, a miniature Doberman pinscher named Sheba, for 50 cents a week. I made another fifty cents a week for feather dusting the shop.

One Fourth of July I got to be in the parade along Farwell Avenue for the shop. Anita put me in one of the old-time, early-1900's dresses. She had to hem it for me (I was only seven or eight). I had a wide-brimmed hat tied with a satin ribbon, a parasol and a baby buggy that I pushed. It had the name of the shop on the sides. I was so happy that day.

I learned a lot from Anita. I got quite an education on my little job in her store. I dusted Greek gods and goddesses and then read about them. All the different kinds of crystals and glassware there fascinated me. I never broke anything, which amazed both Anita and my mother. (I'd never seen my mother use a feather duster, so it was something new to me.)

One section of the shop had old publications, prints and antique postcards. There were lots of reproductions that supposedly were collectables. Many of them had pictures of famous paintings and statues and some of them were nudes. I never asked about or mentioned these discoveries to my mother. She would have said that I was going to hell for talking about such things.

The shop was pretty good-sized, or at least it seemed so to me as I was a kid. The store was about 100 feet deep and at least 30 feet wide. Anita lived upstairs. Some days my mother cleaned there, too. There was a full basement with a lot of antique hardware, crystal, porcelain and ceramic doorknobs, hinges, bath fixtures, drawer handles and all kinds of antique bottles. The main floor was mostly glassware, Depression-era glass in all the colors, and china. They had lots of sterling silverware and serving pieces on display for sale.

Anita was also a professional lampshade maker.

Fourth of July parade, 1951.

She'd make shades out of imported materials, something like cardboard with a grain in it that had real butterflies embedded in it. She'd cut and mold it to the lampshade frame, all custom work for people. Sometimes it took her a whole week to make one. I watched the progress on the lampshades whenever I feather-dusted.

I also got 50 cents a week for sweeping the hair up each night in the neighborhood beauty shop. All these jobs started adding up. The money was a lot to me. Then I had to go home and work for nothing.

We were one of the first families around that got a television when they first came out. Lawrence Welk was my favorite show because they had Myron Floren playing the accordion. I found it fascinating to watch him do all the fancy fingering on the keyboard.

During this era, it seemed every family had an accordion in the house. It was a fad, like the Elvis days and guitars. Salesman went door-to-door, supposedly testing anyone in the household to see if they had enough musical ability to warrant buying an accordion. Of course this was just a sales gimmick—everyone qualified! The salesman gave us an earphone so we could listen to tones and graded our responses on his clipboard. Then he handed the results to my folks for their consideration.

After a few weeks, I forgot all about the music test. Then one day before I went to school, my mother told me to come straight home afterward and not to stop for any reason. When I got there, she washed me up, changed my clothes and made me put on a Sunday church dress and shoes. While she changed, I went outside to play and got my clothes dirty. Was she ever mad! She made me clean up again and change my clothes, all the while mumbling in Croatian.

Then we walked two blocks to Brady Street where she could see the church clock in the distance, which made her step up the pace. We practically ran the four blocks along Brady Street until we came to the Lincoln House of Music. It was a small corner shop that had showcases full of accordions.

My eyes went big as saucers. I was never so excited! Now I realized what the hurry was about. I was to have my first lesson!

My beginner's accordion was a small 12 Bass version. It was a few months before I received with my own red-and-white accordion, a mid-sized 120 Bass, which I'm sure my father bought on time payments. It was beautiful and looked very expensive, not to mention classy.

After 12 lessons, I was left on my own to learn. My dad had size 9 shoes, so I never forgot to practice. The Milwaukee College of Music was just a few blocks from our house over on Lakeshore Drive. They specialized in classical music.

After I learned a few pieces, Dad would take me to his hangouts and belly up to the bar. He'd order his shot and a beer. Then I would play my accordion for the patrons, all his beer buddies. They'd buy him drinks and any cash tips I got went right to him as soon as we got in the car. I got sodas and chips, so I thought we both did well.

One job I found to be a really fast money-maker was gathering bouquets of lilacs from the bushes that grew wild along the hillside near Lake Michigan. The huge apartment buildings along Lakeshore Drive always had doormen who would screen the people entering the buildings to keep out riff-raff and other uninvited visitors. At night, all the doorways were locked and only residents' keys or the buzzer system would let you enter.

I always gave these doormen a bunch of flowers free to take home to their wives. They would slip me into the elevators every time I came by. Then I would sell these bouquets to the residents for a dollar each. The scent of these fresh-cut lilacs, blooming only two blocks away, sold themselves. I often made more than $10.00 dollars a day. I never told my parents about this amazing money-making adventure!

I had a cigar box that I hid behind a loose brick in our basement wall where I stashed my money. It never lasted long!

I was a regular customer at the little Italian grocery store across the street from the playground at Cass Street School. I would buy a frozen Snickers candy bar on a popsicle stick for a nickle and five cents worth of penny candy about three times week. Sometimes I would share with my friends. I enjoyed my frozen candy bar on a stick for two reasons—first, because I couldn't break a piece off to share with anyone, so it was all mine. And second, because it lasted so long. What a deal!

My First Love

I met the first love of my life when I was only 14 years old. His name was Bobby Ray Hoover, who had moved to Milwaukee from Kinston, North Carolina. He was 19 and had beautiful blue eyes, red hair, a great smile and an emerald green pick-up truck. He was polite, and I liked his cute accent. Bobby Ray lived in the neighborhood with some friends from his hometown.

They would all gather on the front porch after supper and sing country western songs. Someone always had a guitar. Many of his friends had other instruments and joined in from time to time. It was fun. The group that he ran with was all from the south. I loved to listen to the country music, even back then when country wasn't cool.

I fell for Bobby Ray and fell even harder when he bought me a ring. I couldn't believe that someone loved me that much. But we had a very short relationship. My older brother, Bob, didn't think Bobby Ray was good enough for me; there was a lot of suspicion about people from the South back then. We had all heard of the scandal of Jerry Lee Lewis marrying his 13-year-old cousin in 1957. And more importantly, there was the five-year age gap between us.

What I remember with the most humor was the excuse I gave my mother the nights I went to meet Bobby. I told her we were going to the lakefront to watch the submarine races. I was sure she believed me. We spent that time necking as we parked, overlooking Lake Michigan.

Things got pretty heated more than once. Even though I knew he had more experience than I did, and as much as I seriously thought about it, I never stepped over that line.

I had two really good reasons. The first was I knew my dad well enough that I knew I wouldn't see tomorrow if I came home pregnant. The other was that I overheard my dad talking about sex to one of his friends. When he said, "Yeah. One time, one baby," I immediately paid attention.

From that day on, I wondered if he said that so I would hear it, or if I just happened to be in the next room by coincidence. Nevertheless, it got my attention, big time. It really didn't matter with the two of us that we didn't go all the way. We had the real thing: true love.

Cuddling, kissing and planning our future filled our free time after the submarine races.

There was rarely a hug or kiss for anyone in our

Bobby Ray

17

household, but I knew my brother and I had a bond that would never be broken. He felt he had to be my protector. Bob had four buddies who remained his life-long friends until he died. He could count on them to help out whenever he had to step in on my decisions.

So I knew Bobby would soon be history. I could see it in my brother's eyes that he intended to break us up. After several months, he got his wish. When Bobby Ray and I realized that it wasn't to be, we went our separate ways with hearts broken. But we had a good time and great memories, Bobby Ray and I!

After my brother broke us up, I would not see Bobby Ray Hoover for almost 40 years. He married a few years later. That only lasted a year or so. The story went that his wife divorced him because he would not throw away his cigar box filled with my pictures and love letters.

At some point, my brother and some of his friends had gotten into enough trouble to end up in front of a judge. This was a hush-hush subject in our house, especially when Bob was given the choice of going to reform school or the army. He chose the army.

While in the army, he found and married his wife, Maureen, a girl from New York. After he was discharged, he went to work at Unit Drop Forge in Milwaukee until he retired.

During these high school years, most of my girlfriends had boyfriends who didn't have a car. A car was a big step up. One day I had to go to Washington High School, clear across town. This was considered one of the better schools in Milwaukee, and I was chosen to represent Lincoln H.S. for the day on a student exchange program to evaluate how that school was different from ours. At the time, I was in Junior Achievement and on the student council.

While my dad was driving me to the school (about 20 miles away and quite a distance to a city person), he gave me a piece of advice I'll never forget. I found myself living by these words, "Remember that there are more than 40 hours in a week, and if you want something bad enough, get another job if necessary." Looking back, I guess I always had that work ethic engrained in me way before that.

A good friend in the high school office, Miss Janet Taeble, also gave me advice. She taught me how to put my priorities in order on payday. Pay bills first and, if there was money left, put half in the bank. The rest? Just blow and have some fun with it!

In addition to working at DeQuardo's pizza, I took another job in a National Food Store. Its biggest competitor was the A&P grocery chain. Even with these two jobs, I still found time for a boyfriend or two.

I took a lot of pleasure spending my money on people I loved. I bought my little brother a brand new three-speed, a fancy imported bicycle. He was about eight at the time. After riding it a few times, there was a mechanical problem, so he took it to a hockshop and sold it for two dollars. My mother didn't do anything about it. I was still paying it off and couldn't believe she allowed him to do that. I just kept paying for it. I didn't enjoy that part.

One Christmas, I bought my mother a full set of stainless steel Regalware pots and pans. To make this an extra-special gift, I taped a 10-dollar bill under each lid and on the bottom of each pot and pan so she could have some spending money that my father wouldn't know about— and something she didn't have to work for.

I bought my father an Elgin watch, about $75.00 dollars back then. He didn't know how hard I was working, or how many hours, and was suspicious as to how I was making all this money. He thought the worst, but only God knows why he never said anything to me about it. I knew I wasn't doing anything immoral. But one day he told my mother to start charging me room and board, $25.00 dollars a week.

I graduated from Lincoln High School in 1962 at age 17, one year after the now-famous Al Jarreau. His brother,

19

Marshall, graduated with me. Incidently, Liberace and Oprah Winfrey also attended Lincoln H. S.

I earned a small scholarship in commercial art. That made no impact on my parents. They thought commercial art was just glorified doodling. The art school thing would have more expenses, so going there was out of the question. In my Dad's eyes, women were here only to get married and have babies. So I looked around for something to do.

Briggs & Stratton was building new plants and hiring people. If you were a country or farm person, they would hire you right off the bat because they knew your work ethic was superior by far to the city applicants. I was a city girl, so I had to go back twice for interviews before I got hired. It paid a lot more money than I had ever made in my life.

Now I had three jobs, including Briggs, where I was making $3.15 an hour plus piecework. I worked at Briggs 40 hours a week, full-time, plus holiday pay. The 35th Street plant employed about 1,000 people. Briggs had about five plants in Milwaukee. I ultimately ended up at the largest one on 24th Street with about 5,000 employees. This plant was so large the building took up about a square mile. It took me about 15 minutes just to walk from my car to the time clock.

Still living at home, I finally managed to buy my first car. It was a used 1959 Ford four-door, an orange-and-white sedan. I decided to buy gas and cruise in my beautiful car. A gallon of gas was the same price as a pack of cigarettes, a quarter. (I never smoked, but a lot of my friends did.) The boys at the gas station all gawked at my car when I brought it in to have them pump my gas, check the oil and see if the tires needed air. I kept that car spotless inside and out, and the guys never even found a smear of grease on the engine.

I knew better than to let my parents know about the car. My brother Bob let me keep it at his house.

Cookie

While I was working evenings and weekends at the grocery store, I was taken with a good-looking guy. He had a nice new Buick and a great smile, but he was 12 years older than me. Hank was so good-looking that I used the family nickname his mother had given him: "Cookie."

As time went on we became friends, then dated, then fell in love and married in 1964 when I was 19. We had the traditional huge Catholic wedding and planned to start a family in about five years. My dad died that same year from sclerosis of the liver at the age of 49.

Cookie was my first, and not knowing "marital relations," I was eager to learn how to please my man. I expected nothing less from him. I read lots of *True Story* magazines and listened for whatever I could learn by eavesdropping on the conversations of my classmates. I was 14 when I found out what pregnant meant. Sex was never a topic discussed around kids. To talk about such a subject was a sin and we believed that we would go to hell for such thoughts.

My mother-in-law was thrilled that her baby boy, going on 32, was finally taking the big step and would give her the additional grandchildren she wanted. She and I got along great. Everyone called her Nona, as did I. Her given name was Amelia.

Nona was a great cook. She made pasties English-style with cubed vegetables, beef, pork, salt, pepper and suet.

21

Wedding bells rang for Cookie and me in 1964.

She didn't use hamburger, like some other versions of the recipe. This mixture was wrapped in her made-from-scratch pie dough and baked at 350°F for about 45 minutes. Crust for bread, meat and vegetables, and juicy gravy from the suet cooking together with everything. It was a very stick-to-the-ribs meal, easy to have for lunch with little mess.

Another one of her recipes was an Italian dish she called stewed chicken that was made with cinnamon. Wow! It was great!

I didn't cook much for Cookie because he wasn't home much except on the weekends. We would have broiled beef tenderloin steaks on a regular basis. I had never eaten steaks before I met Cookie, and I couldn't get enough of them. When I asked my mother why we never had steak, her reply was, "It costs too much."

Even though I knew Cookie wasn't too nuts about kids, a lot of weekends I would get my little brother, John, and he would hang out around the house with us. Cookie's brother had a cottage on Six Mile Lake in Felch, just north of Iron Mountain, Michigan. I took John up there so he could go swimming a time or two. It wasn't much, but I did what I could.

My brother had wrecked my secret car, so I'd been taking the bus to work. I continued to do so after I was married. Then I noticed that while I was riding the bus 25 miles to work in subfreezing temperatures, Cookie was driving his Buick for 3 miles and getting to work in comfort. So I bought a T-Bird. Cookie had a fit. It was a 1964 Ford Thunderbird with lemon-yellow exterior and black leather interior. It was really, really pretty.

A few months later, I remember sitting around the break area at the Briggs & Stratton Factory listening to all the other women talking about their sex lives and wondering what I was doing wrong. The girls picked up on that and gave me some advice that sounded like it would be the answer to turn things around. They told me to take off early one day and get home soon enough to be there while Cookie was still in bed—and then go for it! On that memorable day, I punched out at lunch and immediately felt that I was being watched. I had never taken off early before, except for President Kennedy's assassination, when Briggs shut down all the plants in mourning.

As I pulled out of the parking lot in my car, I wondered if I was doing the right thing. Busybody women, not to mention *nosy*, weren't always the best source of advice. Well, I was ready to try anything at that point. The eagerness started creeping up, and I thought I'd never get home. Lunchtime was no time to be on the expressway—I needed to get home! Traffic was hellacious and seemed to slow down at every exit. If this method turned out to

23

be the answer to my slump, no telling how many times I would go home early.

Full of excitement and anticipation, I quietly climbed the steps to our upper flat, opened the door and tip-toed into the bedroom, where I found my black-haired husband in one of his plaid shirts with his back to me. He was sitting on the opposite side of the bed, leaning over and putting on his shoes or something.

My body was tingling all over as I moved quickly across the marriage bed, came up behind him as he sat there, and grabbed him! I lay him down, kissing him with passion, my eyes closed. He was thrashing around, struggling, and then I heard him say, "Ma'am, ma'am! I'm just your telephone man putting in the extension phone!"

I was dumbfounded as I raised myself off him. He rushed out. That poor man! What he must have thought of me. *This sex-starved woman attacked me*! I was SO embarrassed. Bewildered and stunned, I could hear, just moments later, someone coming up the steps. Cookie.

"Hi dear. What are you doing home so early? Did you see the telephone man?"

"Yeeesss," I said with little enthusiasm in my reply. Needless to say that took care of my hormones for a while.

I dreaded going to work the next morning. All my co-workers were there just waiting to hear what happiness surely had happened. As I told them about my disaster, I started to cry. As tough as I thought I was, this was just too much.

As I raised my head after telling my sad story, you could see how the girls were *really* trying hard not to laugh. Some even had their lips clenched. That lasted only a few moments. Then one of them started laughing, and then they all joined in. They tried to apologize, all the while being doubled over. I couldn't get out to my workstation fast enough. I felt like such a jerk.

When lunchtime rolled around, they all came together and told me how truly sorry they were for laughing after

24

they realized how devastated I was.

I assumed they had a Plan B to help me out.

They did. Well, it couldn't hurt to listen.

It went like this. On the upcoming Saturday, Cookie had the day off. The plan was that I would make him lunch with nothing on but a smile. That would surely be the answer. I went for it.

That Saturday afternoon, Cookie went off to the corner drugstore for his newspaper. I got the beef tenderloin steaks out, seasoned them and put them in the broiler. When Cookie returned, the great smell of broiling steak was sweeping through the hallway. Then he entered the kitchen—and walked right on through to his den. I wondered for a moment if he had even noticed the entirely naked me.

Lunchtime with my "board of advisors" at Briggs and Stratton, 1963.

At that instant, he poked his head around back in the kitchen. He took his pipe out of his mouth and said, "If you weren't so busy making those steaks, we could have a little sex." I replied, "The hell with the steaks! Let 'em burn!"

My advisors were all very pleased—I had finally hit a home run.

Everyone liked Cookie except my mother. She said he was cheap. And maybe she was right. When we went out to dinner, it was on a night the restaurant had a buy-one, get-one-free meal. When we went out for drinks with our friends, he was always the last to buy a round. By then, some of the group had already had enough saving him money.

One of my marital duties was grocery shopping. I also did the shopping for Nona whenever we went to Iron Mountain for a visit, about every four-to six weeks.

One typical weekend, Cookie and I went to the store. I had my shopping list in hand and filled up two big shopping carts for us. Cookie had been reading the paper, looking over the Saturday shopping specials. As I got through the line to the cashier, he met me there and wanted some cigarettes. He'd noticed a price, which was one cent—one single penny a pack—cheaper down the road 8 miles. He tried to haggle the cashier down for an extra penny per pack off. When the cashier declined to give him this great deal, he decided then and there to leave the store to go back 8 miles to the other shop to save the penny per pack. Even worse, we left our full shopping carts behind, right at the check stand.

I didn't say anything in the store, of course. But after we got in the car, I told him that kind of stunt would never fly again, or he'd be doing his own shopping. And I told him how much time and work all that marketing had taken me. It came to nearly two hours that he'd just thrown away without a thought. And we still needed food.

One other memorable time, we were once again in Iron

Mountain. Cookie had dropped me off to do the shopping for Nona. Then he took off to go get his newspaper and tobacco. I loved the smell of his pipe. He looked so dignified smoking it. I had my two carts of groceries paid for and ready to be loaded into the car. This time, there was no Cookie coming to meet me in the store. Finally, I managed to push one loaded cart ahead of me while pulling the other one behind me, and made it out to the parking lot.

Then I noticed our car; he was just sitting there reading his newspaper. I struggled over to the car with the two carts full of groceries. He never once looked up to see if I needed help. I was so mad!

I opened the back doors and loaded the eight bags of groceries by myself, my temper escalating with each sack. Then I took the carts back into the store, got in the car and slammed the door. I couldn't even look at him, I was so mad. I just gave him an abrupt, stern, "Let's go!"

When he finally dropped the newspaper, I turned to him and suddenly realized—this was neither Cookie nor our car!! It was just a white car similar to ours. *Uh-oh!* I couldn't get those carts back fast enough as I apologized to the man over and over.

About the time I got all the groceries back into the carts, there came this gentlemen's wife. He got out to help her with her things while I was struggling to get out of their way. Just at that moment, while she's wondering what's going on, who I was, and what happened, along comes Cookie in our big white Buick. Go figure!

After five years rolled by and still no kids, I decided to split the sheets. I finally realized I would only be a roommate. Five years of my life had been invested in that marriage and wasted. My most priceless, treasured memories were of his family, especially our niece Jenny and nephew Lee.

Being Catholic, we had to go to counseling, which was required when we separated. We were to try to reconcile.

Nobody got divorced. It was okay to break the law, beat your wife or kids, or just about anything else, and still be a Catholic in good standing. But never a divorcee'. When it didn't work, we divorced about a year later.

I made up my mind then and there that I never wanted to marry again. I had to deal with all the remarks after that, mostly behind my back. *What a good man! How could she do that? What about the church?*

I was the black sheep of the family from then on.

Whenever I got irritated at them, I would say, "You don't live behind my doors, mind your own business," or "How dare you?" I was the first in our family to get a divorce.

I wanted kids, even if I adopted them and even if I didn't remarry. Now I was "free, white and twenty-one," as the saying goes. I had a good job and a nice modern apartment. I had a beautiful car and a full plate.

But I wanted a different life, and I was going to go for it.

Learning the Ropes

So there I was in Milwaukee in 1969, divorced and diving into my new life. Only problem, it seemed like there were ten women for every eligible man. Men who could dance were in extremely high demand.

Back then, women were supposed to be subservient and submissive. They were full of such advice. But that didn't stop me. I dated, often several men at a time. Each one was good for something.

At work, we gals wore sturdy work shoes, like tennis shoes or Hush Puppies. Some of the biggest workers' complaints involved foot pain, varicose veins and the like, so Briggs & Stratton put in wood floors at their factories. They used short planks about the size of a cinder block.

On weekends, we loved to get out of our work duds and into dresses. I had a nice wardrobe and hair. There were so many hair styles: beehives, French twists, wash and set curlers! Comb-outs and styling, finished with hairspray! Back then, lots of us wore hairpieces or falls to fill out the hairdo, to make it look like you had more hair. That was the preferred look—lots and lots of perfectly styled hair. A lot of us had wigs for those times when we couldn't get to the beauty shop, or if we wanted to sport a new look, go blonde or something. I had several wigs as well.

I loved to dance and I even danced on roller skates when I was a teenager. You could wear pants, slacks or

JUL 72

Me and my 1969 Impala in Wisconsin.

jeans in the roller rink—stirrups were popular because they were tight to the body and didn't inch up. But for dating, we wore dresses.

In my teen years, I always dated older guys, and we'd go dancing to Glenn Miller music in the big ballrooms. When I was I married, I always tried to find time for music, and I enjoyed all kinds. But Cookie hardly danced at all, so I kind of lost touch with the music world until I dumped him.

Now I had a red 1969 Impala convertible with a white leather interior. I loved it. I also loved the feel of being free with the wind blowing through my hair while on long drives and road trips.

I liked taking my time and looking around, stopping whenever I wanted to. And that was the way my girlfriend and I went to Yellowstone National Park on one of those road trips. My little brother John came along as a surprise to my girlfriend and her daughter, who was also coming. I was twelve years older than my little brother. Lots of people with younger brothers and sisters didn't like hanging around with them, but I wanted to watch John and spend time with him. I took him around with me all the time. Some people even thought he was my own son.

Because I liked to drive fast, I told the kids in back to watch out for cop cars. That kept them busy.

The trip didn't turn out quite the way I thought it would. I ended up getting three flat tires. They started deflating in Cody, Wyoming. They got worn out, one by one, and I had to buy new ones. The tires cost $80.00 each out there, and we were just at the border of Yellowstone park. Nancy and I split the trip expenses, but I had to pay for the tires, so that was an unexpected expense and just about wiped out all my vacation money.

We stayed at a dude ranch near the east entrance to the park outside of Cody. While in Cody, I thought I'd see what the job opportunities were. They weren't paying much compared to the $10.00 an hour I was making back home, though my pay fluctuated according to the piecework. I never wanted to stay in the factory all my life, so I was always looking for a better situation. It was real nice there near the park.

I liked the big trees, the wildlife and the mountains. The trees were huge, the kids got to ride horses, and you could walk through the forest and just let your mind flow. The trees seemed to reach the clouds.

We stayed about a week. If I had found a decent job there, I would have stayed forever, and maybe kept John with me. The whole trip used up my two-week vacation time pretty well.

My first job with Briggs was to check tumblers for various locks to make sure they worked. Almost immediately I became a union representative for the AFL-CIO (American Federation of Labor and Congress of Industrial Organizations). As far as I know, I was the youngest union rep for AFL-CIO in Wisconsin. The thing is, it wasn't a job anybody wanted. If I lost that union job, I wouldn't have the big money. We didn't have job security then. All we had was that day. The health plan and benefits all came later as the union worked things out with management.

I met some other union women at the 35th Street plant who showed me the ropes, such as how to deal with the managers and the board of directors. I became more assertive as they learned people couldn't pick on me. These gals would make me ask the board questions because the board would dismiss a situation if the question came from union people they already knew. I also gathered information that we could use later when we opened negotiations.

It all was pretty exciting, except you became someone on-call, like a doctor, 24 hours a day. I would get phone calls in the middle of the night whenever someone was having trouble with a foreman, or some question had come up and they needed a union rep to help them deal with the situation.

The union got stronger and stronger as Briggs & Stratton got bigger and bigger. And the questions got tougher. I definitely thought that having the union was good because, for one thing, the women weren't getting anywhere near the same pay as men. For instance, some women were flipping these big motors, just like the men, but the guys were getting much more pay. One of the ways Briggs tried to hide this was by putting the men in a different department. But even though we were segregated and separated, we knew that the work was the same.

You couldn't work in the die cast department if you were a woman, but some of the gals were perfectly capable of doing this highly paid work. We women had to deal with a lot of prejudice. We just wanted equality at work. We all wanted to be able to support ourselves and our families, particularly the single gals; not everyone would grow up, get married, and live in a house with the white picket fence, especially with ratios of 10 men to each woman in the workforce.

From 1962 to 1971, I oversaw the work of 600 women and helped organize women's rights along with a team that also helped out with union negotiations. Women had very few benefits at the time just because they were women. Vacations, pay scale, health plan, sick days, retirement, job preference, seniority were all issues where I had a strong part to play. I told women, when men realized what we were worth, they'd appreciate us more.

I never brushed off anything the women came to talk to me about. I went to bat for my gals over anything, large or small. I wrote up grievances for any issue. (Formally, these are called complaints.) Once I even wrote up a grievance that the toilet paper was too rough in the ladies room. Well, it was!

When I worked at the 124th Street plant, the newest and the largest of the five plants, I had already acquired quite a following after having worked at all the other plants from time to time. But I told the women there that I would represent them only if they attended union meetings. I said if I didn't see them there, not to expect me to do my part when they didn't do theirs. In short, I told slackers to take a hike. I don't like people that don't pull their own weight.

Negotiations got more intense. As time went on, I got more and more powerful as a union negotiator. As I got stronger as a leader, I was able to put more pressure on management. And really, it was for the best for everyone.

One day, Briggs installed new state-of-the-art assembly lines. But when the line opened, they just couldn't get the production numbers to go up to where they needed to be. Meanwhile, the women felt they weren't getting enough sick days. The health plan had flaws and vacations weren't long enough. All of this was based on comparisons with the benefits the men got.

Management, all men back then, brushed the situation off because we were just women, and they were sure they could get us to do what they wanted. A lot of animosity developed between the women and management. Now we had an opportunity to make some progress: the reality took about two months to settle in. The new assembly lines weren't producing to their projected potential. According to their tests, these lines could produce *several hundred* more motors per unit of time than they actually were.

That was when Briggs & Stratton called in the union negotiators, of which I was one. This now became our ball game. Money, of course, was a priority. Men were getting two or three times the wages of the women, and the young, pretty new gal that just walked in the door would be given the easiest job. The old-timers with 20 or 30 year's time got the heaviest jobs just because they were old. One could think that the company was trying to get rid of them, but management also realized that the older workers were more experienced and better trained. These were things that had to change, and this new assembly-line situation was our big chance. We'd been after some of these changes for a long time.

Our team then proposed to implement a plan to give the oldest employees the easiest, age-appropriate jobs. With job seniority would come respect, but we assured the company they would not lose production, which was their biggest fear.

With this change and some other improvements, things were getting better, but there were some lingering bad feelings. I suggested to management that they could very easily smooth things over by simply treating these girls with respect. "Give the women respect," I told them, "and they'll give you ten-fold in return." When asked for some specifics, I suggested that they give these gals a donut each morning and see what happened. This wasn't part of any formal union agreement, just an idea that I had. A small investment for what was about to take place.

Next thing you know, trucks full of Dunkin' Donuts showed up the very next morning. What a day that was for both sides! All the supervisors walked the assembly lines with trays of donuts for each gal to take her pick. Production went right up. Amazing how that works!

Things like this opened their eyes and, shortly after that, I was offered a management job. I turned it down because I still wanted to help the employees. Not too much later, I left the job at the end of a workday to find all my tires slashed. We're talking about the good old union days. Companies didn't want powerful unions, let alone powerful women, in their factories. Like all of us on the team, I wasn't just a union rep, but an on-the-job working union representative. I shared the same pay and working conditions as everyone else.

Besides working at Briggs, I did other things as well. My factory workday ended at 3 p.m. For several years I apprenticed at the Victor Johnson Flower Shop, from about 4:00 until 6:00 p.m., four nights a week. I'd got my diploma at the Wisconsin College of Floral Design after several months of night school. To get the certificate, you had to apprentice for a certain amount of time. I wasn't paid, but I learned a lot.

I didn't have much social life when I was single, what with the factory, the union work, and all the other jobs and things I was doing. So, I grabbed what I could. Sometimes I would meet a salesman for National Food, maybe have coffee after work, or go dancing, or sometimes meet for a drink.

Vicky was a good girlfriend of mine. She was older than me, a single mom with two kids. For a while she was working at another factory, and she didn't make as much money as she could at Briggs. So she came on over to Briggs & Stratton and ended up as one of the gals in my department.

Vicky knew I had recently been divorced, and she thought I was putting in too much work and not enough play into my day. One day she came to me with what she thought I needed—a remedy. "You need some fun!" she said. She had one particular guy in mind for me. I assured her that I had a social life and gave her some version of, "Thank you very much for your concern."

I didn't want her help.

But Vicki wasn't listening.

The Art of Dating

Vicky didn't give up. The more we talked and the more she found out about me, the more she wanted me to meet this one guy. And the more she insisted I should meet him, the less I wanted to.

I had this boyfriend at the time who was a manager at the gas station behind the Milwaukee Arena; he didn't have a lot of time on his hands. He gave me free gas, free oil changes, and free parking at the arena if I wanted to go there. He was one of several guys I was dating. The attitude that I had developed after my divorce was that all men are good for something, but each is not good for the same thing. I wanted fun, and this guy was fun.

He had all the stars, wrestlers, basketball players, etc., come to his station because he let them use it to park their busses when they performed in Milwaukee. He was invited to many of the after-event parties that I also attended. At one point, I even got a press card through him and was able to go back stage. I could also take friends and family to meet the celebrities. Fun!

Vicky kept insisting that I would enjoy this one particular gentleman friend that she knew, the one she had so firmly in mind for me. She let me know that he was well dressed, a very successful car salesman, nice-looking, and, oh yes, he played the concertina, a squeezebox. Also, he had a little band and loved polka music.

Although I played the accordion and loved the music, I also had a huge love for country music. Music is something in my blood. My father had played the

Backstage with country music legends Tex Ritter, June Carter, The Statler Brothers and Charlie Pride.

concertina, and I had taken those accordion lessons. Vicki knew that and was sure this concertina information would get me out of what she called "my shell."

The concertina is commonly referred to as a squeezebox, or just box, and has four rows of buttons on both sides of the instrument. It is a very hard instrument to play. I know this because I tried to teach myself. I learned to read music while taking 12 lessons on the accordion when I was a kid. I had inherited my dad's sheet music, which is used for both instruments, and went through it, looking for the easiest pieces to start with.

Each key has a number above the button to coincide with the number above the note on the sheet music. As you press a key and pull the instrument out, you get one sound, but if you hold your finger on the same key while pushing the box back in, the sound will change. The sheet music has little icons above the notes, coding whether you should be pulling or pushing the bellows.

These instruments are common in many European countries, such as Ireland, Italy, Germany and Poland. The Star Concertina Company in Chicago made some of the finest boxes of all. I had one of the best, made by the owner himself. His name was Wally Kadlubowski, Jr. of Mount Prospect, Illinois.

Star Concertina in Cicero, Illinois, near Chicago, was the last factory to produce Chemnitzer-style concertinas. Star Concertinas go back to 1917 when three craftsmen formed the International Accordion Company: Walter Kadlubowski Sr., Walter Mojsiewicz and Kajetan Perkow.

In 1926, they decided to make concertinas and incorporated, with Star as their trade name for the instruments. Star eventually became the largest concertina manufacturer in the country. Walt Jr. followed in his father's shoes, starting as an apprentice.

Concertinas can be played standing up, sitting down or while you stand at the bar. Many players use a neck strap while they're playing. Concertinas are manufactured in

My custom-made concertina

different keys, the most common being G. Good players can transpose keys to any tune. Not me.

Vicky couldn't get me to go on a blind date in any way, shape or form. So she plotted to get me to go out with her in another way entirely.

My days were very full. It started by getting up at 5:00 a.m., driving 25 miles to punch in at work at 6:30 a.m. and work until 3:00 p.m. Then I went to my apprentice job at Victor Johnson Floral Shop four days a week from 4:00-6:00 p.m., then worked part-time at the National Food Store near my home from 7:00-10:00 p.m. Surprisingly there was still some time for me to enjoy the nightlife; I didn't need much sleep.

On my free days, I enjoyed taking lessons on shooting pool. Lessons were available for a fee at the Milwaukee YMCA. The game fascinated me. Even though I was the only female there, I found myself acquiring a passion and becoming quite good at the game. I loved the strategy, planning and control it takes to win.

I played a lot at Pal Joey's, a nearby bar with some of the best men pool shooters around. Sam Scaffidi was my teacher, advisor and friend. He knew I had what it took to put up a tough challenge in the main competition. We would use Pal Joey's for picking the toughest opponents to practice on and ultimately beat them.

I found myself practicing shots as much as three hours at a time. Because going into a tavern and shooting pool was an unwritten no-no for women, and of course you were going to hell if you did it, I enjoyed the game even more. Men of all ages, walks of life and color were more than happy to show me their best shots. I entered several tournaments, both singles and doubles, did quite well and ultimately won a state championship in 1969.

I was usually the only woman in the pool hall, and I often practiced one shot for up to three hours.

41

Vicki didn't rest, even though I turned down her invitations week after week. Finally, I thought she got the message when she missed a weekend of approaching me with the next great opportunity. A week or two later, when I saw her coming toward me with a big hopeful smile on her face, I started walking in the opposite direction. She shouted out to me, over the noise in the factory, and I had to stop and listen so there wouldn't be a scene. She assured me that she just needed a favor.

What was this favor, I wondered?

She had always wanted to have a reading by a fortune-teller and finally decided to see one. She wanted me to go with her. She made it sound like it was really important that she have someone with her, especially since it was a long way away. She wanted me along for the company and to keep the secret in the event she got bad news. I could see that she seemed to be very serious, so I said yes.

I met her at her house after work that day at about 4:00 p.m. When I got there, she let me know that she was getting ready and wouldn't be too long. I waited for a while outside, listening to music in my red convertible and finally got impatient.

I tried to hurry her and that's when she let me know she was stalling. When I asked her to explain, she told me that she had invited someone else to go with us. She said she couldn't get me to go out with him any other way and just as I was getting ready to hop in my car and leave, around the bend came the reason for her stalling. He drove up in a new white Chevrolet.

"Icy blue eyes," Vicky said, trying to sell me on this guy. "He's about 5'8" or 9. Very wiry, slim," she said. "But older and bald, with just a hint of some curly hair left. Ten years older. His name is Art."

I was livid. But now I was stuck. As she was telling me all this, the man in question was pulling up to greet us. *That guy! He was going bald!*

"I don't want some old bald guy!" I told her.

"When this is over, I'm going to kill you."

Vicki had a smirk on her face, happy as hell that she had finally created a meeting. Even though I was forced into being polite in this situation, she knew very well I wasn't pleased. Now she hurried us along, saying that we had just a little time to get to the fortune-teller. Vicky rushed to get in the *back* of Art's car and nudged me into the front *with him*. By this time, I doubted this fortune-teller even existed. She promised me that she indeed had this reading booked and the fortune-teller was a man. So, of course, she needed someone else to be there with her.

Since I was already in the car, I tried to get my temper under control. I had already cleared my plans so I could go wherever it was Vicki and I were going. I thought I would just make the best of it, but I also thought what a waste this was, infringing on my quality free time.

As we drove south out of town, Vicki introduced us, telling me a little about him, his music and playing the concertina, and told Art a little about me and that my dad had played the concertina. He asked his name. I told him my father was Pete Pestka, from the Hatley, Wisconsin area. Art replied that yes, he had heard of him. I immediately thought, *"Oh, right!"*

Then it seemed like every person Vicki or I asked him about was someone he knew as far as the music world went. I thought he was pulling my leg big time. Everything now was going in one ear and out the other.

I was just enduring all of this.

The drive seemed to be going on way too long. Vicki agreed, but reassured us that it wouldn't be too much longer. The distance seemed much farther than it really was. It turned out to be only about 50 or 60 miles. We finally arrived.

One by one, we paid our $5.00, which was a lot of money to me, and had our fortune told through a card reading. At the time, I was thinking this is all a bunch of bologna. Vicki went first, then Art. They both were amazed at what this guy told them. Then it was my turn. When I got in there, he flipped the cards and with each flip, told me a little fact or something about me. I'd never heard of a male fortune-teller. Who could figure?

My future was to include a long trip, a new relationship with a handsome, blonde, blue-eyed guy, some kids and a place with a white picket fence. The American dream, right? Well I'd already tried the American dream— my marriage to Cookie—and that hadn't worked out so great. Then we all piled back in the car, comparing what we each had heard. We were all surprised with what the fortune-teller had come up with for each one of us.

As we started back to Vicki's, and still evaluating our futures, Art said, "Why don't we take a little break and have a drink?" He knew a place. We agreed to stop, as we were still scratching our heads on how this guy could know so much about us by reading cards. Actually, he really didn't read them, it was more like he just shuffled them around.

As we entered the little tavern, Art was greeted at the door, and then he introduced us all around. Art was the only guy in the place who was wearing a suit and tie.

While we were waiting for our drinks, Art started the conversation ball rolling by telling a joke. I'll never forget this one as long as I live: "How does a Polack pull up his socks?" Everyone asked, "How?" That's when he dropped his trousers, bent down, and tugged on his socks.

While everyone else buckled over with laughter, I turned beet red with embarrassment and was disgusted with someone I had just met being so uncouth. The spectacle ripped it for me. Vicki was trying to shush me, as she could tell I was ready to let Art have my opinion of him with both barrels.

Art tried to change the tone at the table. Maybe he noticed he hadn't made such a great impression on me. He spotted an old broken-down accordion on the back bar and asked me if I would play a tune. He said that if I was the

44

daughter of a Polish dad, I surely knew some Polish tunes. I assured him, rather stiffly, that I knew several. That's when he asked the owner if I could play everyone a tune.

Vicki was grinning; I told myself again that I would kill her. To get me to play, Art promised me after that we would leave. So then I thought, great! That was a good deal!

I strapped on the dusty relic, leather straps tattered and frail with age, and started to play one of the Polish favorites. Art had stepped behind the bar and started putting up liquor bottles side by side on the bar, in a long row. He took two cocktail mixing spoons and started to make music by clanging them between the bottles and running the spoons back and forth from bottle to bottle. As each bottle was a slightly different size with differing amounts of liquid, each sounded a different note when he tapped it. It was obvious he had done this many times before and also knew these people at the bar. I had to admit, the bottles, played like a xylophone, sounded really good.

Art smiled at me. I turned around, looking for Vicki, only to find a tall good-looking gentlemen standing next to her. Sometime during our stop at the tavern, she had called her boyfriend, Hank, to join us. Or maybe he'd been told where to meet us.

I calmed down quite a bit after a few drinks and the good music. I continued to play a few more tunes and, after a while, I realized Vicki and Hank slipped out. I'm sure Vicki thought leaving me stranded with Art would solidify her matchmaking plan. Now I was out in the middle of nowhere. There were no cabs and I was left with a guy I had little use for.

I decided to just be patient, and I would get back home sometime, some way. Just another good reason to choke Vicki for dumping me to go off with Hank. People liked the music and I always like that. I bided my time, enjoyed being the entertainer, trying not to scowl at Art.

Finally, he motioned to me that he was ready to leave. On the way back to town, he offered to take me to a nice dinner club called The Rafters. I decided to make the best of it. As we talked at dinner and in the car, I had a few more drinks. I decided that this guy wasn't too bad, although I was still angry with him for pulling that stupid joke.

There were several dance hall bars in Milwaukee. Sure enough, Art suggested that we stop along the way back and dance. A man who could dance back then was a big thing, very desirable. If he was any good, the gals wouldn't leave him alone. I loved to go dancing, but I didn't have much time in my schedule to do it.

So I thought I would check him out to see what kind of dancer he was. I wasn't disappointed. Then he wanted to go somewhere else when he realized I knew how to dance.

I thought I would try to dance him into the ground. I wasn't going to get my way. At the next stop he opened the trunk of the car, pulled out his concertina and brought it into the bar. Now I was curious to see how good he really was. While we waited for our drinks, he showed me again that he knew the operators and let them know he had his concertina. They urged him to play. So he did, and everyone loved it!

After a few more places and a few more tunes, it was closing time, and I finally ended up back at my car. I was glad to be back in control of my own whereabouts, but thanked him for, what turned out to be, a not-too-awful night after all.

Art asked me out again—so the both of us could play music and see how our instruments sounded together— but I passed. I thanked him and let him know that I was in a relationship. Then I went on my way.

Thinking over the whole crazy adventure as I was driving home, it actually had been fun. But I spent most of my time thinking about what I was going to do to Vicki when I got a hold of her. I wouldn't see her again until

Monday at the plant.

I worked my other jobs on the weekend and spent time with my boyfriend. When I arrived at work on Monday, Vicki was there, dying to hear how everything had gone. After I chewed her out big time, I told her. She wondered when I was going to give in and not be so stubborn and date him again.

"Not going to happen," I assured her. Now that the air was cleared, I went back to my usual full routine.

About mid-week I got a call. Guess who?

Art.

Would I like to go out?

"No, thanks, I have other plans."

After being so short with him, I thought that he got the message. I kept thinking about that whole afternoon and weekend, and suddenly I was mad at Vicki all over again.

Art loved wearing my wig
to cover his thinning hair.

How did *he* get my phone number? It had to be from Vicki!

Saturday rolled around and the phone rang at 9:00 in the morning. It was a very soft-spoken man who introduced himself as Father Jim of a Catholic church on the west side of Milwaukee. He sounded very sincere when he told me that he listened to confessions the night before, and that he was very concerned about the mental state of one of his parishioners. The man had just gone through a very nasty divorce. After trying to get this gentlemen through months of consoling, he could see that someone had suddenly made a difference.

I listened to him. I, a divorced Catholic myself, had dealt with pain. Father Jim then asked me for my help. "How could I help?" I asked. Then he let me know that it was Art he was talking about and asked if I would just visit with him over a cup of coffee or something. Nothing more. And it would not only help him, as a concerned priest, it would also help Art through the hard time he was going through.

He seemed so desperate for my help that I agreed to meet with both of them that afternoon out in Muskego, Wisconsin, on the outskirts of Milwaukee. It was a beautiful day. I always loved putting the top down on my candy-apple-red Impala convertible. It took about 45 minutes to get there. I had to drive through the city and into the rural, dirt roads of Muskego. I really enjoyed those days of letting my hair fly in the wind.

When I got there, Art seemed surprised to see me. I didn't see the priest. We said our hellos and went into the cafe that was our meeting spot. Then I heard a loud, noisy rumble. It came from a huge Harley motorcycle. Looking out the window, I saw a tall gentleman get off the hog. He was coming into the cafe with a big smile. Art introduced me to his friend "Father" Jim. They laughed as they let me know that it was all a joke and that it was all so Art could see me again. (Jim Bonney was one of Art's buddies.)

What a guy! Jim offered to give me a ride on this great-looking bike. I'd never had a ride on a motorcycle before, and it had lots and lots of chrome. We buzzed around the area and came back to the cafe about 15 minutes later to find Art was gone. Jim told me to get in my car and follow him. Sure enough, as soon as we pulled into the parking lot of a bar facing beautiful Muskego Lake, I spotted Art's white Chevy.

When I got out of the car, I could hear polka music. As we entered, there was Art and his concertina and, as before, he was playing it on the bar. Everybody seemed to know Art. As I talked to the people listening to the music, I realized this place was also a ballroom where many dances were held. Lots of boats were docked outside. Guests could also buy boat fuel here. Needless to say, this became another day of road running and music. I had to make a few calls to clear my plans. My excuse was that something came up and I'd have to take a rain check.

Saturday afternoon ran into Saturday night. I didn't get home until the early morning hours of Sunday. This was a day that I always welcomed. I slept until noon that particular Sunday, which was a first in ages. Instead of washing my beautiful car on Sunday morning, I got it done at a carwash. Instead of making breakfast, I went to George Webb's. This made up for about three hours of chores I normally did on a Sunday morning. I went over to the gas station to get my tank filled and to see my boyfriend, Dick, and spent the rest of Sunday with him.

Art would come up with the darndest excuses to get to see me again. One time he told me that he wanted me to go to a big party with him at a fine cocktail lounge in one of the nicer hotels. I told him it was out of the question. I had been out with him the night before and my hair was a total mess. I wouldn't be able to get ready in time. He assured me that it would all work out because he made an appointment at a nearby beauty salon to save me the time and allow me to attend. I agreed, as he was the one who had messed up my hair so badly the night before. Since I desperately needed a new "do," I thought, *"All right—he's paying for it."*

He gave me the address of the salon, which was no problem to find. When I got there I realized he had pulled another little joke on me. The name of the beauty parlor was CURL UP & DYE. When I went in, my hairdo was already paid for, and they did a good job in time for me to meet Art at the party. Everyone was dressed in business suits and upscale attire.

I'm glad I went. These types of events were right up my alley. I liked to look nice, dress nicely, and do things that would open doors for me. I had as many pairs of shoes as I had outfits to match.

But Art was a real joker. Another time he called me to go out to dinner. He asked me to wear something especially nice because he wanted to take me to this great place to eat. He reminded me he would be on his lunch hour, so to please don't be late so he could have as much time as he could with me. I got all dressed up, my hair looking great (sometimes it had a mind of its own), and got there in plenty of time for his lunch break. He drove my car and off we went. Guess where?

He took me to a drive-in root beer stand for the hotdog of my choice. Was I ticked off! All that preparation for a hot dog. That was Art for you.

When we left the drive-in, I drove. I wanted to keep him from returning to work. I parked a few miles away. Then I started making passes, but Art just wanted to talk, nothing more. He needed to be back at work because he had clients booked to look at vehicles. He finally figured out that I wasn't going to take him back, so he took my car keys and started walking.

I went after him, still wearing my spiked heels. As he walked faster, so did I. At one point, he started running so I had to take off my shoes to keep up. I was used to running short distances and figured I'd poop out this old guy shortly. To my surprise, he disappointed me and ran all the way down Bolivar Avenue until he lost me. I used some choice words and returned to the car to lock it up.

I knocked on doors until I found someone to give me a ride to the dealership. Art was with a customer, and didn't see me. I slipped into his office, found his keys in his coat pocket and drove his car home. Later that night, Art showed up at my house with my car, mad as hell. He got over it, eventually.

Vicki was still in the picture, keeping up on the latest that was going on with Art and me. Her boyfriend had a little tavern called "Hank's on 6th," and we frequented this place quite often for two reasons. He liked my music, which I enjoyed playing there, and there was a good group of regulars. Hank's tavern also had a pool table.

I hadn't forgotten what Vicki had pulled on me, getting me to agree to go to the fortune-teller, and that she and Hank had left me stranded with Art. They thought it was funny. But what I was going to do to them would be *really* funny. Even though now I was seeing Art, I needed to repay them. So I did. I put posters up on the shop bulletin board that there was going to be a free luncheon at Hank's that Sunday and every Sunday from then on, right after church.

Hank did this for his regular customers every Sunday, and that particular Sunday there were so many people waiting to get in when the doors opened, that the line of people backed up outside and extended around the corner. It was weeks before the news got out that I was behind it.

At last, I was even with both Vicki and Hank.

Pranksters in the Woods

Art and I had fun wherever we went. Good fun.
Things were even too good. He had a girlfriend and I
had a boyfriend, and still we always found time for us to
play music together. We continued to see each other, no
strings for him or for me. I needed to get out of what was
becoming a too-close relationship.

This one Saturday night my boyfriend Dick asked me
where I wanted to go after dinner. I suggested a place
called the Sparrow Club, where there was dancing. I also
knew Art was playing there with his band. When we
arrived, the band was just bringing in their instruments
and setting up. Art was at the bar having a drink. Looking
around, I noticed a drop-dead-gorgeous slender girl
with long, flowing, beautiful dark hair, hauling in Art's
concertina, amplifier and stand. All the while, Art lounged
at the bar with his drink.

Remember, here there were about 10 available women
for every man. They were very submissive and in many
cases paying their own way just to have an escort. This gal
was about 15-to 20 years younger than Art and seemed to
be content just being around him, doing anything to be his
girlfriend. Let me tell you, that would never be me.

At the same time, my regular boyfriend was no slouch.
He was very nice looking, had money, made sure my
car was serviced, and he loved to dance. After a while, I
started dating another guy named Daniel Topchezski, who

also loved to dance and happened to be from my dad's hometown of Hatley.

His nickname was "Big Don." He was very tall, which I liked. He was a comedian and a better dancer than either Art or Dick. He spent all his money as fast as he made it, mostly on me. I liked that too.

It was hunting season, November 1970, when I took a trip to Hatley with him. His sister and family were at his mother's and visiting from Alaska. We all hit it off. A lot of it had to do with my dad being from Hatley and my knowing the polka music and style of dancing.

Back then, women were supposed to do all the cooking and cleaning. Even during hunting season, women were stuck at home while the guys would hunt from early morning until sundown. (I didn't know about all the fun, jokes and drinking yet.) Hunting was sounding pretty interesting to me. Half the crew would wait at a convenient spot in the woods so someone could shoot any deer flushed out. The other half would drive the deer in their direction. At the end of the hunt, the meat would be divided among all the hunters.

I had no intention of cooking and cleaning when I had a chance to go hunting with six guys, including Big Don. There was Eddie, Jumbo, Jose, Jerry and Gerome. This sure didn't fly with their women. I didn't really let their reactions concern me—I just sat back and let Big Don handle it; after all, I was his girlfriend.

I had a new .30-06 Remington semi-automatic rifle, a new red flannel shirt and hat, Red Wing boots and wool socks for the hunt. My hunting buddies didn't mind my being along because they had new blood to pull their jokes on. The first thing they did was to put me on a stand (a clear spot in the woods) for a snipe hunt. Since I had never hunted or shot a rifle before, I didn't ask any questions. I didn't want them to think I didn't know what I was doing. They claimed they would check on me now and then, but of course they had no intention of returning after they left.

As we walked into the woods, the sun shimmered through the treetops. This gave me a peaceful feeling as I was preparing to trap my snipe with a gunnysack, deep in the north woods.

The trees were still full of leaves. It was so thick that you could barely see any light through them. There was a mist hovering over the snow-patched ground. It was so pure, it was almost spiritual watching the mist, kind of like a fog. By now it was getting *really* dark, and I had no clue how to get out of the woods.

I finally realized I'd been the butt of another joke, so I started hiking. I crossed over a frozen creek covered with snow, as was the area I was walking through. I don't know how long it took me, but eventually I made my way to a road.

After I had walked about a half a mile, a farmer picked me up and told me what a snipe hunt was. Needless to say, there is no such animal. When I asked where these guys might be hunting, he said, "The nearest bar," holding back a good laugh. I had him drop me off at one and there they were. Boy were they surprised to see me.

Don's friends complimented him on his choice of girlfriend. I had impressed them. For being a city-slicker gal, it was fun to change lifestyles for a while and adapt so quickly. Now that I was one of the guys, it was time to have some fun. They told me some of their hunting secrets, especially how to keep warm. The remedy was very simple: a pinch of snus and a swig of ginger brandy. What else would one need?

We all had hunting licenses, two of which were doe tags. After the first day of the season, only one deer was taken, a buck. After each drive, which took about an hour, we would move on to the next hunting spot. There always seemed to be a tavern where we would stop, have a touch of kindness, and compare hunting lies.

On the second day, the guys perched me up on a knoll to have a clear shot at any deer they might push through.

My hunting buddies.

A little later, sure enough, here they came, about 10 of them. I had no scope on my rifle. The deer I aimed at had the biggest horns, I mean antlers, I'd ever seen. The more I stared, the bigger and longer and sharper those antlers looked. Now it was headed right for me!

Steady. Steady. Now—shoot!

I shot. Ker-BOOM!

A hit! Down it dropped. I walked over to admire my trophy. Then guys arrived and began complimenting me on the nice shot. Just one little surprise—there wasn't an antler to be seen. It was a huge doe! I just acted cool. No big deal.

This was my first deer and all my buddies were proud of me. They couldn't wait to tell everybody, especially the women in their lives. Later, Don took my doe to a taxidermist to have the head mounted.

The Hatley Hotel was one of my buddies' regular

stops. A gentleman named Bernard owned it. We all walked in, and he couldn't wait to tell us about *his* luck. He had taken a huge eight-point buck. Being with guys that were full of mischief and fun, I could see the wheels already turning. They enlisted me to start the ball rolling.

I asked Bernard where he had this huge deer and if I could see it. He told me he had it hanging in his garage behind the hotel, and after he served everyone drinks and finished his work, he would take us all to see this magnificent animal. In the meantime, two of our crew slipped outside and then secretly swapped his deer with my doe. Time for the fireworks.

Bernard couldn't help bragging as we walked out back to the garage. Then with a flourish, he proudly opened the double doors only to find—what's this? —a *doe* hanging where his prize *buck* should have been. He about had a heart attack, he was so mad! Of course, I had to act stupid, per my instructions, and ask him where this deer's antlers were, then ever so sweetly say that I thought all bucks had antlers. He fumed and stomped out of the garage, then went back into the hotel and called the game warden.

Time to activate Phase Two! My next job was to keep him busy while the guys swapped back the doe with the buck. This was getting good.

The warden finally arrived and went back with Bernard to check out his complaint. There was the buck, hanging right where it was supposed to be.

"O.K. Bernard, just what's going on here?" asked the warden. More sputtering. Then the warden accused Bernard of drinking way too much and not to bother him again with any more such nonsense.

Another time they took me to the local bordello called the White House in the nearby town of Antigo. Madam Ella and her White House Bar brothel were so infamous, they were famous. The gang decided to have some fun, starting with making me look more like a guy. They dirtied up my face, had me tuck my hair under my hat,

56

and rolled my sleeves up so my long johns would show. In we went. We all bellied up to the bar.

We were just reaching for our first drink when I was approached by one of the gals to go upstairs. I answered, "Sure." They immediately knew by my voice that I was a female. *Jig's up!* They quickly grabbed for everyone's drinks, which some of the guys got to first, and showed us the door pronto. We could barely walk out standing upright as we were so weak from laughter.

The weekend was coming to an end and now it was time to go back to my city life. Later, I heard that Don had to pay double to have my doe head mounted. The taxidermist told Don that the only doe he'd ever seen mounted was by a buck. But finally he relented and said he would do this under protest, and only because it was my first deer.

Big Don and I went together for a few more months. I had him play Santa for my nieces and nephews, but ultimately we went our separate ways. Things were also thinning out with Dick, the guy with the gas station near the arena. All the while, I was getting closer with Art.

Back at the factory, it was time to turn in my request for vacation time. All the girls I represented also had to turn in their requests. That's when my girlfriends and I decided on a group vacation to Acapulco. We all got approved for the vacation dates we wanted. We were all set!

As time went by and it got closer and closer to departure day, one by one all the girls dropped out. I would be traveling alone. Now what?

For about a year, I had kept a page from the Green Sheet, a section of the *Milwaukee Journal* that had a picture of Alaska in it. There was a small log cabin, and in the background, some mountains covered with snow. It looked really nice and peaceful. The photo was taken in Wiseman, a tiny settlement about 100 miles north of Fairbanks. Population 12 and the only way there was by airplane!

*This picture of a cabin in Wiseman, Alaska, kept me
sane while working in the factory.*

I put this picture up in my workstation at Briggs &
Stratton. Whenever the pressure from the union job got
to be too much, whenever one of the girls was hanging
around complaining in my ear, I'd threaten to go to Alaska,
right there like in the newspaper, where it was peaceful. A
lot more peaceful than this huge factory I worked in.

Going to Acapulco or going to *Alaska* would cost
roughly the same. Hmmm.

I decided to call Big Don's sister in Alaska. I liked
Louise, her husband and their three little girls, and so I
asked if I could come visit for a week.

"You can't come for just a week," she said. "Alaska is
way too big for a week."

"Well I have a two-week vacation," I told her.

"Then we're going camping," she said.

"Do you think you're up to staying in the woods?"

In the woods? *My idea of camping was staying in a Winnebago and theirs was camping in a tent.* But I didn't know that, yet. I would find out this and many other things were different in Alaska.

I planned the trip for the end of June through the first week in July, which I later extended by another week after Louise explained that one week wasn't really enough time.

When I told people where I decided to go on vacation, they thought I was joking. This was a big change from my original Acapulco Beach plans with my girlfriends. *The women in the Midwest just didn't get it. They were afraid of being different, afraid of trying new things or of making mistakes. How would you know unless you tried?*

It would take 15 hours to get to Fairbanks by airplane. The routing was Milwaukee-Minneapolis-Seattle-Fairbanks. A round-trip ticket in 1971 was tremendously expensive, right about $550.00 plus tax. Extra luggage, after two check-in bags, was $15.00 each.

I had never been to or read anything about Alaska and thought it would be an adventure. Whenever I thought of Alaska, I envisioned polar bears, ice and snow, mountains, dogteams, gold panning and, of course, igloos.

Destination Alaska

After departing Billy Mitchell Field Airport in Milwaukee, I questioned the stewardesses about the price of drinks on the plane. The mixed drinks were a dollar. Just so you know, from Milwaukee, Wisconsin, to Fairbanks, Alaska, it was only six Bloody Mary's away.

We flew right over Mount McKinley. I could only see the top of it through the clouds and I just got two pictures of it. I wasn't too impressed with it until I was told I was only seeing the top. It looked like an iceberg rising above a bed of clouds. When I arrived in Fairbanks, I noticed the baggage waiting to be loaded included racks of antlers, moose and caribou, rifles and hunting gear.

For a moment, I stood at the door of the plane before I went down the stairway to the tarmac. I looked over the spectacular snowcapped mountain range while breathing the fresh air. It only took me an instant to realize that this is where I wanted to spend the rest of my life. It was a beautiful, clear, warm day, the mountain ranges were picture perfect and the air was so clean. I said to myself, "If I can find a job here, any kind of job, and even just exist here, this is where I'll spend the rest of my days."

With my accordion strapped on, I made my way down the steps and played a little tune as I entered the terminal where John, Louise and their three girls greeted me. The kids were about 8, 10, and 12 years old.

I was disappointed as I looked around the airport

because there were no igloos or dogsleds in sight. But I figured they must be somewhere nearby. The natural beauty was breathtaking, but it was the air that really did it. The clean, pure Alaska air. Those were the days of factory smokestacks and lots of automobile air pollution back in the Midwest. (It took me three days to adjust back to the air there after I returned. Sometimes people just don't realize what they are breathing.)

When I had talked to Louise about coming, she told me that the weather was about the same as Wisconsin at that time of the year. To me, that was eye-opening because everyone pictures Alaska as the land of ice and snow. It actually gets hot in the Interior in summer, up to 80-plus degrees, and the Interior of Alaska was where I was going.

I had enjoyed my long plane ride to get there and, after the little tune I played for them in the terminal, I had to tell everybody about the hospitality on the flight. Mini-skirts were in fashion then, and Alaska Airlines had just revamped their stewardesses' uniforms to reflect some of Alaska's Russian heritage. The ladies now wore very short red tunic-dresses and tall bearskin hats. They served us a beverage called Russian Tea, which came wheeled down the aisle on a cart in a huge pot called a samovar. It was about a three-gallon unit, brass-colored, very ornate, beautiful and different. The tea wasn't bad either.

The first question John asked, "What do you want to see?"

"Polar bears," I replied.

Since I had not done any research on Alaska beforehand, I got educated fast that polar bears were out of the question unless I wanted to spend another $600 or so to go to Nome or Barrow, approximately 1,000 miles away. So that idea got put to rest for another day.

I remember the population of Fairbanks was about 15,000 with another 15,000 in the surrounding area. About two percent of the people in the area were Alaska Natives: Inupiat, Yup'ik, Athabascan and Aleut. There were a lot of interracial couples too.

The main drag was, and still is, Airport Road. This road only had a few businesses on it, one of which was a much-needed Sears catalog store. On the other main street, there was a J. C. Penny's and an F. W. Woolworth's Five and Dime. It was all very surprising to me to see those familiar retail names out in the middle of the "Land of Ice and Snow" where I was enjoying summer temperatures comparable to Milwaukee. Plus we had about 22 hours of daylight compared to only 15 back in Wisconsin.

There was one campground in the area called the Norlite Campground, and that was where we stayed for the first night while the Grys' family showed me around. (Norlite is still there and currently rated eighth on a list of 15 specialty places to stay in Fairbanks.)

The highlight of Fairbanks to me was Two Street. This was two blocks of door-to-door bars and shops. Some of the bars had a walk through to the back entrance of the bars whose main entrance was on First Street. I couldn't help but notice all the activity on the pool tables and all the good-looking guys playing pool.

At one point, I looked in the phone book to see if I recognized any names of any people who could have been relatives. My mother's family name is Stefanich, which is close to anyone whose name ends with -*vich*. The phone book was full of **"Viches."** Stephovich, Butrovich, Haedokovich, Yankovich, Jackovich. I immediately thought, *Wow this town was full of Viches.*

Oh yes, even the famous Frankie Yankovich, "the King of Polka Music," made his way to Alaska. (He wrote the *Blue Skirt Waltz*, which I played with him in Fairbanks. Frank had taken an old Bohemian melody and worked it around a bit with a lyricist. It became a hit after it was recorded in 1949. More than four million records and recordings of it have been sold through the years. One of his boys married a Native girl and they had four children. It was so cute to see four little Native kids that could do the polka. (They were good too.)

As soon as I got into the car, a big Chevy Suburban, with Louise and her family, I began to see how different life was for her kids as opposed to the way I'd been raised. The girls had no limits as to what they were allowed to do, and they just seemed to do anything and everything. Sliding down the hill on a piece of cardboard, no helmets. Sometimes the terrain was treacherous, but they just ran all over the place.

Back home, people were more cautious. At meals, the Grys' kids got to sit with the adults and even shared in the conversation. That was a little annoying to me, although now I understand why they were allowed to do so. They were pretty spoiled, but at the same time they were good kids. I don't think they realized how good they had it.

It was hard for me to get a laugh out of John; he was solemn-faced all the time. He loved my music, though.

Everything was an adventure to me. I found out what it was like to camp outdoors and to sleep in a sleeping bag, make food and cook it on a campfire. We used river water to wash our faces and do dishes. All of us used the woods when we needed the bathroom. All Alaskans carried a roll or two of toilet paper in their vehicles. (Oh hell! We still do so today.) This kind of real camping was something I'd never done before and I found that I liked it.

Just about 14 miles south of Fairbanks on the Richardson Highway (Alaska Route 2), we stopped at North Pole. Not the geographic North Pole, which is actually 1,700 miles north, but the little village of 265 people named North Pole.

The post office here would postmark any cards, packages or mail with their entirely legal imprint of "North Pole, Alaska." We stopped next at the world-famous shop, Santa Claus House, and I got my letters mailed to all my nieces and nephews straight from "Santa." Of course I also sent one to my little brother, John, who was then about 14 years old.

Post office at North Pole Alaska.

Those girls! When we were camping, they would go right to where the garbage was in these campgrounds and try to find old bottles or other treasures. Once the littlest, Caroline, came back with a bottle that had a dead shrew in it and she didn't want to let go of it. John had a heck of a time figuring out a way to get that shrew away from her. Lorraine was the middle child, and Cindy was the oldest.

I got to taste kippered salmon along the way and to eat Dall's sheep meat, which still remains my favorite meat today.

With the ratio of 20 guys to every girl in Alaska, as well as the beautiful clean air, I had already decided that this was the place I wanted to spend the rest of my days. *Alaska.* Just saying the name made me feel wicked good.

The whole way that men looked at women up here was so different from Wisconsin. Back there, women worked hard every day just to feel presentable to men. Everything they did, everything they wore, how they did their makeup, EVERYTHING was designed to make themselves stand out among all those other gals trying to catch a man. But all the standing-out had rules and limits. Most women were afraid to eat too much, talk too much or laugh too much, whatever too much was. They were self-effacing, which I could never stand.

Here in Alaska, a good appetite was looked at as healthy. I'd always felt that I was a little chubby, although I never had trouble getting men. But it was nice that up here the whole idea that I might have to worry about an extra pound or two was ridiculous. No one cared. Everyone was active and busy and the food was wonderful. I brought my host and hostess some eggs and tomatoes, as fresh food was hard to come by in Alaska. I also brought them some fresh cheese curds and some Wisconsin summer sausage.

Also, a woman didn't have to labor over her wardrobe to get male attention. Up in Alaska, if I wore a short-sleeved blouse, it was considered wild. If I wore a V-neck, that was wild too. I didn't have to diet and be skinny and wear a bikini to get male attention like in the Midwest.

The Healy Hotel was right on the Alaska Railroad tracks and had housing for some of the railroad guys and any guests coming in by train. They had a café and a bar, with two pool tables. A black gal, Francis Davis, was the swamper there. She did all the housekeeping and I always treated everyone the same. It wasn't really of importance to me, but it was to her.

In the early days, there weren't many black people in Alaska. There was no visible, open prejudice; we knew we were in the land of misfits and we worked with each other. No open vicious hate like was possible *Outside*, the term Alaskans used to refer to the other states. There might have been hidden stuff with some people, but I didn't give prejudice the time of day.

Discovering Alaska

I had to get used to the whole new concepts of *road* and *highway*. Most of the roads were gravel except some in Fairbanks and Anchorage. Also, most of the roads in Alaska had only two lanes, one each for opposing traffic. About every 50 miles or so there was a roadhouse, an all-in-one facility that would have rooms for rent for the night, some food, a gas pump and a bar.

John drove most of the time. We were on the Richardson Highway (also known as Alaska Highway 4). This was the first major road built in Alaska. For a long time it was a pack trail that ran from Eagle to Valdez. The U. S. Army built it in 1898 to create an American route for prospectors to reach the Klondike gold fields in the Yukon. Following the Fairbanks gold rush in 1902 and the construction of a telegraph line a year later that paralleled the trail, it became the major way to get to the Interior of Alaska. In 1910 it was upgraded to a wagon road, a project led by Wilds Richardson, a U. S. Army general. The story goes that unsuccessful gold miners were hired along with regular construction workers so that those who had "gone bust" could earn enough money to pay their way back home.

Paxson Lake was one of the most memorable stops, located at Mile 185 Richardson Highway. It was enormous, clear and still had snow mounds that were so high the kids couldn't wait until they could slide down them using a

*The Grys' girls play in the ice
at Paxson Lake in June.*

flattened cardboard box and a large plastic bag for sleds. It
was eye-opening to see snow and ice deposits on this lake
at the end of June in 75-to 80-degree temperatures.

Whenever we stopped at any of the roadhouses, we
wouldn't go in until I strapped on my accordion. John
would hold the door open while I played a polka as we
entered. And he did it with a straight face, too.

Everywhere we went we were welcome. I was told that
I was like a breath of fresh air. It didn't take long for me to
realize Alaskans were free-spirited people. People were
hungry for good old-time music and in some roadhouses
you could even find a polka or two on the jukebox. There
was music and fun to be had by all.

One of the stops was in Talkeetna where we looked up
some friends of the Grys'. Susie and Jim Keller and their
children were sure glad to see the Grys family, and their

four kids were glad to see the Keller family children. The great distances between settlements and time-consuming travel on gravel roads meant visits were seldom unappreciated.

Talkeetna was a little village with only about 200 folks living in the area. It was about six blocks long with a post office, VFW, roadhouse and a few small businesses. Many buildings were old and made of logs. There were several small airplanes that seemed to be more plentiful than four-wheeled vehicles. This, I found out later, was the way it was throughout the state; many people had planes so they could get around.

After the introductions with the Kellers, they learned I had an accordion. We all agreed it was party time. With the Kellers as our escorts, off we went. The Grys' girls stayed home with the Keller kids. We drove with the car windows open, and my music could be heard all along Talkeetna's main street. We ended up at a nice place with a piano, the Rainbow Lodge. I played music until closing, which was about five in the morning.

Even then, we were still going strong, but the only place still open was the A-Frame Café (called the Teepee today and still operating). I was never so close to being kicked out of a place than I was that day. The crabby gal that ran the café wasn't too happy with my good old-time music so early in the morning.

One of the natural wonders when I visited was the lack of darkness, even when the sun was down for a few hours. I never wanted to go to sleep! I had all kinds of energy. Louise always put foil on the windows wherever we slept to keep the light out.

As we traveled, I learned that even though the bars closed at five in the morning, they could reopen at six. I guess the hour closed gave the owners time to count their money and swamp the floors.

One thing was pretty obvious and that was the appetites and the good food wherever we went. The year I visited, a resident hunting license allowed each hunter five caribou and two moose. That was amazing to me. In Wisconsin, the limit was much, much lower. The roadhouses served wild game buffets all the time so I got to try several kinds of wild game and fish.

Dog teams were another thing that I wanted to see. Like so many people, I thought I was going to visit a place that only had ice and snow. If Louise hadn't warned me, I might have packed only winter clothes.

Mileposts were another new experience. These were upright posts that showed the distance from the start of the highway. It was pretty neat to go along the highway and figure how far it was to the next destination. Then I noticed another highway marker of sorts. They were tall pole-like structures that had an extended arm at the top reaching over part of the road. They measured snowfall and also guided the snowplows in the winter. There are places, such as near Valdez, which have so much snow that it is sometimes impossible to drive.

Now we headed towards Healy along what is now called the George Parks Highway. As we drove the 150 miles, the altitude increased from 346 feet at Talkeetna to 1,344 feet. There were many places to view Mount McKinley. What a sight! It was immense, not at all what I thought it was when I first saw it from the air.

There were several spots along the way to fish. The rivers were crystal clear, and fishermen were pulling in fish one after anothr. Animals were plentiful and we saw lots of them including moose, caribou, fox and an occasional wolf or two.

After a long stretch of gravel road, we stopped to see the only igloo of my entire trip. This structure was a wood-framed building at Mile 188.5 Parks Highway near Cantwell. It was still under construction and was planned to be a huge hotel with about 50 rooms, a bar and dining room. It was enormous and built in an area about a hundred miles from any settlement. The gas, at one of the two pumps, was the only thing you could purchase along with a few items such as oil, candy or soda pop. (The Igloo was never finished and was never opened because it didn't conform to any building codes. It is still there today.)

Cantwell was the next stop. There was a reindeer experimental farm operated by the University of Alaska. Reindeer and caribou looked exactly alike to me, and they are genetically considered the same animal. The difference is that caribou are wild and reindeer are somewhat domesticated. The reindeer were controlled in a fenced compound and were fed a balanced diet.

Cantwell is the settlement at the crossroads of the Denali and Parks Highways at an altitude of 2,212 feet. Here you could find gas and lodging. It was a designated stop for the Alaska Railroad and had a post office, liquor store, landing field and aviation services. The restaurant

I finally got to see a sled dog team at Mt. McKinley (now Denali) National Park headquarters.

boasted that it was open all year and the supermarket claimed it was the largest in 200 miles. Only about 60 people actually lived there, but the services were handy for folks driving to Mount McKinley National Park. Cantwell was at Mile 210, and our next stop was Healy, at Mile 249, and the Grys' home. We passed a lot of little places with funny names like Mindy, Yanert, Moody and Garner.

The road to Healy had a lot of curves, sometimes with rivers following the curves and sometimes with mountains on both sides of the vehicle. Occasionally there was a view of the railroad tracks. The Alaska Railroad connects Fairbanks with Seward, a distance of about 470 miles.

The railroad is the main means of transportation for the people living in remote cabins. The train will stop for anyone standing along the tracks waving a jacket or hat. (This is called a *flag stop*.) Depending on how many times this happened, a trip could take many hours. The train had a club car. The conductor would greet you, sell you a ticket, and assist you, if needed.

When I rode the train, I noticed my conductor's watch chain was loaded with gold nuggets spaced closely along the links. Gold was about $40 an ounce. Very expensive. Alaskans were partial to gold nugget jewelry. Nugget watchbands and rings were very common. Some of the miners would make up capsules called *bezels* of different sizes, the largest being about the size of a half dollar and filled with the dust from their finds.

It was late by the time we got to Healy and the Grys' home. The Grys family was Catholic and welcomed the traveling priest about twice a month. Masses were held in a community hall. The parishioners would share responsibilities and duties the remainder of the month.

All the buildings in the settlement were pretty much the same brown color. Going down the hill into Healy was very scary to me. It looked like the road was falling straight down. Looking around, there were mountains, the river, railroad tracks and a bridge crossing over to a huge

71

power plant, all huddled in this little nub of civilization. There were a few families, but men made up most of the population.

Louise was the Healy postmaster. Her post office building was metal, about 20 by 20 feet. It had about 70 mailboxes in it. Their school had a small enrollment and was made of trailer units pushed together. It had all grades with as few as eight kids to a classroom. There could have been more than one grade in a room. Cantwell high-school-aged students were bussed to Healy. The roads between the two settlements were very narrow in places and treacherous, even in the summer months, not to mention dusty.

There was another settlement across the bridge called Suntrana. It had a small school with children in grades 1 to 6. Older kids went by bus to Healy, about 10 miles away. Suntrana had the power plant and also is the location of the Usibelli Coal Mine, the largest coalmine in Alaska. Usibelli shipped coal as far as Japan. They were making history with a purification system that filtered the smoke clean before it was released through the stacks into the air. They also brought in the largest crane in the country, if not the world. It was big enough to drive a full-sized pick-up truck into the bucket.

Healy, like Talkeetna, was a railroad town with lots of workers. They were housed at the Healy Hotel. There were three main places to go: the hotel, with rooms, cafe and bar; Otto Lake Lodge, with a bar and food service; and Paul's Roadhouse, with a bar, food and lodging. There also was a gas station selling snacks and food.

There was one payphone in Healy. It cost about a dollar a minute to call Milwaukee from there. I remember getting $10.00 worth of quarters and calling my friend Art. When he heard all the quarters being dropped, he joked and said he thought I was calling from Las Vegas with all the *ding-ding-ding* sounds.

I told him I needed more money because everything

72

*I just loved this hand made fur parka
that I discovered in Healy.*

cost so much. I wasn't spending much, but I hadn't taken
much to begin with. Even incidentals were expensive.

I was also thinking about buying a beautiful handmade
fur parka that I'd fallen in love with. Back then, many
people in Wisconsin would never dream of wearing a fur
parka even though lots of people trapped and sold fur
for extra money. I could tell that fur and skins were the
warmest clothing and excellent for windbreaks in the cold
weather. The Native lady who had sewn it wanted $600,
but in the end, she wouldn't sell it to me. So, I didn't need
so much money after all.

There were about 20 guys for every girl. I thought I
had pretty good pickings for sure! John and Louise had
fun hauling me around and introducing me to everyone.
Then I would play music to entertain. Once again, I was
like a breath of fresh air. Even though there were a lot of

good musicians around, including guitar, mandolin and fiddle players, there were no squeezebox players. I have to say, the music sure sounded great. These instruments really compliment each other, especially in a laid-back atmosphere with musicians playing songs that everyone knew and then having a drink to top things off.

Then I would play an occasional game of pool to see how good these guys were. The tougher they were, the better I liked beating them. They didn't know that I had played a lot of pool in Milwaukee and even won a pocket billiard tournament in 1969.

Back then, it was considered a sin if a woman would dare go into a pool hall, and if we shot pool, we would surely go to hell. Therefore, women rarely shot pool back then, and if they did, they had quite an advantage over the men. This was even truer in Alaska. It seemed like I always had a line of guys waiting to play their turn with me. I always called every shot and my game of choice was Eight Ball.

Between the pool games, playing music, doing a little flirting and drinking as many drinks as I could handle, I always had a pretty full day. Women could not pay for their own drinks in a place because there were so many men willing to treat them. I always had at least one dance partner. However, I lost out on a lot of dancing because I was also playing the music.

I did notice something. Alaska, the land of the wild and free, was also the land of the misfits, as I found out more than once. As my conversations got longer with people, I found out that some of the folks around here were running from the law, ex-wives or ex-husbands, bills or the IRS. The list was endless. Nobody seemed to care why someone was here and everyone was more than eager to help you if you needed it.

Everyone also had a backyard full of treasures (which we city slickers usually just call *junk*). It wasn't very easy to get to a parts store of any kind, so everything was saved for the proverbial rainy day.

I also noticed that the women didn't fuss much with make-up and hair-dos. The gals helped each other with their hair for special occasions because there were few beauty parlors or barbershops. You would have to go to Fairbanks for a professional. People in the rural areas were the "Jacks and Jills" of all trades and made do with what they had to work with. That really appealed to my nature. It was very apparent to me that everyone was happy with the simpler-is-better lifestyle. Nobody was above anyone else and keeping up with the neighbors didn't seem to have a place in Alaskans' lives. I liked that.

The Alaska Railroad ran trains daily through Healy. Passenger trains ran only one day a week going north and one day a week going south. The daily trains hauled general freight, fuel, coal and logs. People could make a bulk order of groceries from Fairbanks, have it put on the train and dropped off on the next southbound train to Healy or any other rail stop. This was done quite often. This sure was proof of frontier living to me.

Catalogs could be found just about everywhere, mainly Sears, Penney's and J. C. Whitney (especially for truck parts). Catalogs were a way of life for most of the other shopping people needed to do. The post office served as the daily chat room. Everyone had to pick up their mail because there were no mailmen for door-to-door delivery. If you stuck a mailbox out on the highway, the mail truck would leave your mail there. This kind of rural area delivery is still operated the same way today. It's kind of like walking back in time.

There was only one TV station and very little radio reception. CB radios were a common way to communicate, but you could not get a signal in many places because of the interference from the mountains.

John was the foreman of the Healy area railroad stops. He got railroad housing as part of his pay that included a small two-bedroom house with a kitchen, living room and full basement. There were very few houses in town and the power plant employees lived in most of them. This was my introduction to an ongoing problem in rural Alaska—the lack of housing.

A number of employees of the Usibelli Coal Mine lived in trailers at Suntrana, closer to the mine. Some employees purchased houses in the surrounding areas. Property, when available, was very reasonable. A number of people brought trailers in and leased ground from Usibelli for long-term set-up. Some residents wanted to live closer to the school.

The owner of Paul's Roadhouse was from Wisconsin too. He offered to show me around. When I found out that it would be by way of his private airplane, I accepted. There were several small planes tied down in the parking lot next to his business. They were all either Piper Cubs or Super Cubs. This roadhouse was located just about six miles south of Healy.

The small plane that we used for my sightseeing was a two-seater. We flew in and out of this canyon and zoomed down low for an exciting closer look.

There was a fascinating canyon just south of here. You could see a rushing river, called the Nenana, with high cliffs of glittering rock loaded with fool's gold. There was a narrow winding gravel road and railroad. We spotted dozens of animals such as Dall's sheep, wolves, moose, coyote, fox, caribou, lynx, wolverine and lots of grizzlies, not to mention many smaller animals and numerous species of birds.

I thought the ptarmigan was the most unusual bird of all. It looks like it has furry feet, but they are actually covered with small feathers. Ptarmigan feathers turn color as the seasons change from warm to cold. It looks like a spruce hen in the warm season, but it turns pure white in winter. The ptarmigan is the state bird of Alaska.

Then we flew over to a dinner club several miles north of Healy. As we circled the club, I wondered how far we would have to walk from the nearest airstrip. Little did I know that we would land right on the gravel highway! This kind of plane-to-door service was common. There were many, many planes left in the restaurant parking lot. Several homes had airstrips right on their property.

The dinner club was called the Tamarack Inn and had a reputation for being the finest dinner club in Alaska. People came from all over the state, often flying in for just a few hours to enjoy the fine food and atmosphere. It was owned by Pat and Vic Rentschuler. He was a retired colonel from Clear Air Force Base, which was about 20 miles away.

Paul ordered a captain's plate, a huge platter with all the finest seafood of Alaska piled on it. Here I tasted scallops, king crab and lobster for the first time. I was always a steak eater and finicky about tasting most anything else, but that night I gave everything a try.

After dinner on the way back to Healy, I got to land the Piper Cub. I was so excited that I was shaking a little. I didn't know that back then landing was considered the most dangerous part of flying an airplane. When I touched down, the big balloon tires cushioned the many bounces and eased my insecurities. The hair on my arms stood straight up. I actually had landed a plane! Go Girl!

What an achievement—to me this was the life. Alaska was definitely a free-spirit destination where anything could happen. I saw that people worked hard and played hard. This was growing on me by leaps and bounds. So far there wasn't a thing that I didn't like.

However, being from a big city, I found myself being picky from time to time. Food was the thing. I had to make up my mind that I would try to eat all these different kinds. Moose meat was more common than beef. Caribou was another substitute for beef. Black bear was served instead of pork. For all intents and purposes, I tried everything even if it was only once.

Honestly though, who had time to eat? After being

in Healy for only a few days, I had made a lot of friends. When Judy, the bartender at the Otto Lake Lodge (Mile 120), found out I was going to be in town for my birthday, she let everyone know and it was party time. Twin brothers Doug and Dudley Yordy owned the lodge and loved old-time music. And boy could they dance! With polka music on the jukebox and me on the accordion, away we went.

While I was dancing with Doug, his twin brother was making a batch of spaghetti for everyone. I peeked into the kitchen to find Dudley with a drink to one side and a pot of noodles cooking on the other. As I watched, he reached into the pot and snaked a noodle out. Then he threw it up to the ceiling to see if it would stick; that meant the pasta was cooked. As you could imagine, the ceiling had an array of spaghetti up there for cleanup. When I asked him about that, he just said, "Who cares?"

Today I was hitting all the places to celebrate. With only a few days to go before the end of my vacation, I had made some good friends and had a reason to return. I was not looking forward to leaving Alaska, but knew that I would return someday.

Paul was buying me all the drinks I wanted at his roadhouse. He sure seemed happy to see me when I would come in. I thought it was because I could hold a crowd playing music and shooting pool. It also helped being a single girl, the new girl in town. I soon found out that he loved me and wanted to marry me. We were all drinking a lot that night and so I said, "Sure, I'll marry you." I didn't love him but thought since I had married once for love and it hadn't worked out, if I ever were to marry again, it would be for money. It looked like he was a man of means, so I agreed.

When it was time to leave, I returned to Fairbanks by train because the Grys' were both busy working again. Their vacation time was over and so was mine.

Burning My Bridges

When I got back to Milwaukee, Art picked me up and I burned his ears with all the excitement in my voice telling about my trip. As we walked out of the baggage claim to get his car, I couldn't stop coughing. It was the air—polluted with smoke from stacks at the nearby factories! It took about three days to adapt to that dirty Midwest air again. By adapt, I mean not coughing every single minute.

Art told me he had always wanted to go grizzly hunting. He was hungry for all the news I could tell him about Alaska. Just the name *Alaska* has a certain magic to it and stops people from whatever they're doing to hear what is being said. This remains true today.

When I got back to work, I started selling off my things to people I worked with. The rumor got out to management that I was quitting. I got called to the office of Mr. Big Shot, Vern Soxx. As I entered, he greeted me at the door and then asked me if I was planning on moving, as he put it, to the "Continental Divide." I assured him that I hadn't decided to make that move as yet. In the back of my mind, that would be a wish come true for him.

He was the CEO of the largest plant Briggs & Stratton had. He was the one giving the order to have Dunkin' Donuts brought in for the women. Not having me to deal with would be a huge relief for him and the rest of management. I'm sure they said, "Here comes trouble," whenever they saw me coming. It was common knowledge when I headed toward the office, I meant business and had an issue to discuss and deal with.

When I left the office, all the girls were dying to hear what went on in there with Vern. I didn't want to burn any bridges just in case things didn't work out. So, with that thought, I smoothed things over for the time being. Very few people knew what my plans really were, let alone believed me if they picked up any gossip. *Who would ever think of moving to that God-forsaken land*? was the first thought of many, especially my family. My good friend, Beverly Krolnik (now Henry), never doubted anything I did or told her I was going to do. She knew I was a go-getter and never looked back.

Everyone I knew was a packrat of sorts. Beverly was one of the best packrats I ever met. We had so much stuff we never thought we would ever have to part with. Was I in for a rude awakening when it came time to choose which of these treasures I would take with me to Alaska and which I would sell. What I thought had great value quickly diminished as time went on and my tentative departure date was approaching.

There were so many things I had to give away, store or throw out, and every day was closer to my final day. It's just a shock what little material things actually mean to you when you have to pick and choose what to take, knowing your life is due for a major change. It is amazing how possessions can lose their meaning.

My good friend, Judy Kocent Freeman, had a hard time dealing with my leaving. I also had another friend, Lolita Arbuckle, who didn't believe I was leaving for good. Paul and I exchanged letters for weeks after I returned. My plans were firming up. As mid-September rolled around, I had most of my things spoken for.

Things seemed to be falling into place. Now it was time to tell Art that I made up my mind to leave for Alaska in October. He listened, but I know that he didn't think for one minute that I would really go. It wasn't until I told him about Paul and his proposal that he thought I might do this, but only as a maybe. With phone calls and letters, Paul let me know that he decided to come to Milwaukee for a visit. His mother was still alive, so he would also visit her in Rhinelander while he was in Wisconsin. I was to pick him up at the airport.

When the day arrived, I received a call from another friend whom I desperately wanted to spend time with. He was visiting from out of town. I agreed to meet him that night when he got in. In the meantime, Paul was to arrive at the airport that afternoon. Now things—these guys—were squeezing in on me. As I made my way to the gate to meet Paul, I stopped at a payphone to call Art. Looking down the aisle toward the gate, the passengers were deplaning. And there came Paul!

He sure looked a lot different than I remembered. I was on my own turf now and I decided right then and there that this marriage he wanted would not work. I knew that he was not somebody that I wanted to look at every morning for the rest of my days. Before I could say anything discouraging to him, he gave me some presents. He had gold nugget wedding bands in hand and a pair of homemade, smoke-tanned, beaded sealskin slippers.

My first thought when I saw the bands, was *yuk!* If I were going to get into another marriage, I would expect diamonds, BIG ONES, from him or anyone else. And as far as the slippers went, they smelled of smoke and who knew what else. Maybe they were tanned in urine! To this day, I won't wear slippers of any kind. I like the feel of bare feet while relaxing.

At that point, the most important thing was to set things straight. I knew my face would show how I felt, so I waited a moment and thought what I could say. Diplomatically, I told him that it took some time and distance to realize that I couldn't do this; I couldn't marry him. I wanted to be honest with him and let him know that I didn't love him.

What I said hit him hard. Shocked by my response, we talked for a bit. We left the airport with a plan that I reluctantly agreed to. He thanked me for being honest with him, but he still wanted me to come to Alaska. He promised me a job, lodging and asked me to date him only for six months. If at the end of this time, if he couldn't change my mind by then, there would be no hard feelings. I agreed to go forward with the move. He told me that he would buy me a truck to haul my things and he would drive it, by way of Vegas, up to Alaska.

That was not going to happen. After realizing this union was not happening, there was no way I would let him buy me a truck, let alone drive it and me to Alaska. I told him he could help me pick out the right truck for the trip, but I was going to buy it and drive it myself. I tried to convince him I needed this time to clear my thoughts, especially after being recently divorced and approaching a new milestone in my life. This long drive by myself would give me the time to weigh my thoughts. I had no intentions of being obligated to him under any circumstances.

As we made our way to the car, I knew that he was thinking that I had my own apartment, and he thought that I was going to have him stay there. I had no intentions of letting that happen either. So I took him to meet my mother.

She told him that there was no need to find a motel and that he could stay in my old room. I thought that was the perfect remedy to my situation. I left him with my mother, and I went out with my friend George from out of town. I apologized to Paul and told him I had a meeting that couldn't be helped, and I would see him in the morning. I know he had other things on his mind, but I had no intentions of any hanky-panky with him.

Right now I had a lot of guys to juggle. Maybe too many. I had Paul on the line, Art, my gas station owner (Dick), and George. I had no long-term plans for any of

82

them, but I wanted to take advantage of what they could do for me. My mother didn't help matters because she thought I was sinning just because I was divorced. I was an embarrassment to her because I remained the only divorced one in the family.

I had a wonderful evening with George and said my good-byes to him. I told him I was moving to Alaska. We decided *For the Good Times* would be our song.

When I picked up Paul the next morning, I could see that he wasn't too happy about being dumped at my mother's. This wasn't his idea for his first night in Milwaukee. Oh well! We went sightseeing for the afternoon and then went to see Art. When we got to the car dealership where Art worked, he was busy with a customer.

We looked around the lot and the showroom until Art was free. I introduced him to Paul and they began talking trucks. We decided that I could do this trip with a half-ton, two-wheel-drive pick-up. I could have a camper shell made for the bed with a drop door that locked to haul my stuff and get head-bolt and pan heaters installed These heaters were necessary because vehicle engines had to be plugged in to heaters during the winter months when the temperatures dropped well below freezing. This kept the engine oil from gelling in temperatures of -30°F or colder.

This was all new to me. I had never heard of such a thing and neither did a lot of garages that I asked to install them. With these heaters, I could feel assured the truck would start in the sub-freezing temperatures I would likely encounter in October on the road to Alaska. Eventually, Art found a garage that could do the job and another guy to build the cap for the truck.

Art sold me the truck for $100.00 over cost. When he got me alone, he told me that if I was really serious about this move, he would even come over and help me load the truck. I made the deal for the truck and extras and off I went. I had one thing left to do. That was to learn how to

My new truck without the camper shell.

drive a stick shift. I had no clue, but how hard could it be?

After we left the dealership, Paul and I made plans to leave the next day for Rhinelander, his hometown about 250 miles away. I met his relatives and enjoyed my time there. I took my accordion and played some music for them. I also went along with the story Paul told them about marrying me. What could it hurt? I left him there that night and when he came back to Milwaukee, I took him to the airport. Everything was rapidly coming to a close in Wisconsin.

Everybody and their neighbors were giving me lessons on how to drive a stick shift. I was jerking, lunging and jumping all over the place in my new truck. After awhile, all the lectures on how to drive were not one of the things I wanted to deal with. I avoided any more offers of help.

I was really getting antsy to take off. Getting the shell was the only thing holding up the trip. I had sold everything I could and stored my car and anything else left over at my mother's. I told her to sell whatever she wanted and keep the money because I was never coming back to stay.

Wall-to-wall carpeting was big in those days. Having a little bar in your living room was the thing to do. No one, absolutely no one, could understand why I was giving up my apartment and all the things I had just sold, just so I could go to *That Godforsaken Country* as they called Alaska. No relatives or friends could understand either when they heard that I was packing up or selling all my belongings.

Mom's boarder told me that I should take a handgun for protection and gave me his pistol for the trip. He didn't know that I already stowed my .30-06 Remington semi-automatic rifle behind the front seat of the truck. He preached that anything could happen to a woman traveling alone. I had no fear of anything at that time. I thought of just taking my time, stopping whenever and where ever I wanted, doing what I wanted when I wanted, answering to no one, and playing pool or music along the way. I never thought anything bad could happen.

Boy was I wrong.

North to My Future

Art and I went out a few times before I left. It was very hard, as our bond grew stronger and stronger. At first we brushed off our relationship as lust and passion, not realizing we were developing growing feelings of respect and love for each other. He covered up his feelings by pulling stunts.

I found out that he was making bets with his friends that I would barely get out of the state before I would change my mind and be back. He did hold to his word, however, and helped load the truck. He and his friend, Al Martens, came over, Art wearing a suit from work and Al wearing everyday clothes. Guess who did most of the loading? There was so much stuff that the back of the truck sank very low.

A lot of the things they loaded was gear I purchased to resell for double what I paid once I got to Alaska. I had kept my eyes open when I was visiting there and watched the prices. There were no chain stores or bargain stores there in Healy or anywhere else. Sorel boots were the main item I bought for resale. I paid $25.00 a pair in Milwaukee. Catalytic heaters, about the same. These were going to be my bankroll, my nest egg, when I sold them. More than half my truck contained resale items. I had a lot of flower design items, household things, my instruments and clothes. Pictures and scrapbooks were my most treasured possessions, along with my mounted doe head, carefully placed in the front seat with me.

I had a beautiful concertina specially manufactured for me that I was now learning to play. I told the salesman that I wanted the most expensive one that they made because I didn't want to lose interest in it. I thought that if I should ever just leave it sit in the corner, for example, I would look at it and say, "I spent too much money on you to let you sit there," then pick it up and play some more. I didn't have a teacher, so I taught myself. I always said I can play like a pro for about 20 minutes, and after that, if you should stick around, I would be in deep do-do.

Now, I had everything loaded, had said all my good-byes, had the truck checked and double-checked at the shop and by the boys at the gas station, and purchased maps. I also bought the famous travel guide, the *Alaska Milepost,* for that year, 1971. I had about $500.00 cash for the trip, back-up oil, snow tires, a good radio and time. What else would I need? I was all set.

I had good weather the day I left. I took off right after Cookie came to give me a good-bye kiss. I got on the expressway and took Highway 94 West. For the first time, I really looked at the scenery. I knew I wouldn't miss the factories and the traffic. I enjoyed seeing farms, beautiful wooded areas, lakes and, closer to Eau Claire, fantastic rock formations. I headed toward the twin cities of Minneapolis-St. Paul. That was the first leg of my trip. So far, so good.

The next day I headed toward Fargo, North Dakota, and I ran out of gas on a Sunday. It was like they had rolled up the carpet and shut everything down in that small town. I finally had to stop at someone's house to ask for help. This was only the second day. I knew I had to get more organized, and fast! I was still in civilization and already in trouble.

On my way once again, still jerking the truck from time to time as I wrestled with the clutch, I spotted signs that said "Weigh Station Open. All trucks must stop." So of

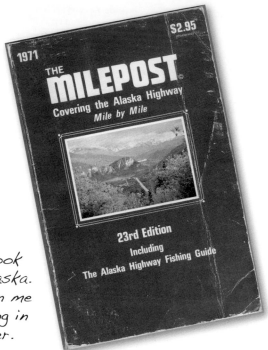

The 1971 Milepost book that guided me to Alaska. Too bad it didn't warn me what to expect driving in the middle of winter.

course I stopped. I had no idea how they were going to weigh this truck of mine. I was afraid of what they would say to me. I knew I had more than a half-ton of belongings packed in my truck and was afraid that I would have to pull some of my things out and leave them. Boy, was I relieved when the agents got a good laugh and told me this scale was for semi's and sent me on my way. I had never driven a truck before, let alone on the highway. What did I know? I was back on the road again, stopping wherever I wanted.

The roads were all good expressway so far. I overnighted in motels that usually cost about $30.00 a night. I tried to drive about 500 miles a day. That was good enough for me. So far, I wasn't looking back except to wonder how Art's bets were going and whether someday he'd tell me.

My next destination was Bismarck, North Dakota. Then I headed north on Highway 83 to Minot where I spent the

night. I pulled into a huge truck stop/dinner club, got a
bite to eat and filled up with gas. In those days attendants
pumped the gas and checked your oil and tires.

While I was having dinner, I noticed a piano in the
dining area. They were rolling it into the dinner club for
the evening. After I ate, I asked the waitress when the
music would begin and who to talk to about getting a
room for the night. I went into the lounge after dinner and
waited for the music. When the pianist began, I asked if
he minded if I joined in. He said that would be great. I
brought my accordion in and the fun began.

As the evening went on, the crowd took up a collection
for me. I guess I looked like I needed money. Here I
was dressed in jeans, my Red Wing hunting boots and
red flannel shirt. Everyone else there was all dressed up,
the men in nice suits, the women in cocktail dresses and
wearing lots of jewelry.

I didn't want the money but the owner told me to
take it. I suggested using it for my room. That was out
of the question, he said. My room was on the house, as
was usual for musicians, and so was my breakfast the
next morning. Some of the dinner staff worked the next
morning and let me know how much fun they had singing
the old sing-a-long favorites, one after the other all night
long. With that, I was on my way.

The next stop was the Canadian border. Now here was
another thing I knew nothing about. I was asked for my
driver's license, insurance and how much money I had. I
also was asked how long I was going to stay in Canada.
After checking my truck and rifle, they let me through. I
knew I had to change some of my money to Canadian,
so at my next stop in Estevan, Saskatchewan, I found a
bank and changed $200.00 for Canadian bills. It was sure
a shock to me. Their money was all different colors, a
different color for each denomination. It looked a lot like
large-sized Monopoly money.

I was in for a rude awakening almost right off the

bat. I found myself stepping back in time. The road I had taken near the town of Estevan (which may have been a detour, or so I'd like to believe) led me to a single lane dirt road. I had no way to turn around, as trees hovered over the top of my truck and I couldn't use my mirrors to back up. I could see cross traffic in the far distance ahead of me, so I kept going forward. To my shock, which left me bewildered on what to do next, I had to stop for a river. It looked like there was no way to get across. Where was the bridge?

With no way to back up, at least with my knowledge of stick shift driving, I sat there stunned, shook up and very nervous. Thank God it was daylight! Shortly thereafter, I faintly heard bells that seemed to be coming closer. As I looked for them, I realized they were on a motorized barge that was approaching the landing I now saw on the riverbank.

This fellow manning the barge motioned for me to drive closer to the river. I was scared and thought I could make a wrong move and end up swamped in the water. The boatman said something in a funny language to me and motioned again. Then with broken English, he came up to the truck and said that I must drive the truck on the barge. For a fee, he would get me to the other side where I could get back on the highway. I asked him to put the truck on the barge for me and he agreed as other vehicles had now arrived behind me and were waiting to cross too.

The driver behind me translated what the boatman had said. It was Canadian French and fun to listen to, but getting on the barge was scary. The hair on my arms stood straight up as I sat beside him as he drove the truck down the riverbank and onto the barge. "No problem," he gestured as he spoke a few words.

Four vehicles were taxied across the river. I was never so glad to get to the other side. Once I got back behind the wheel on solid ground and back on the road, I slowly regained a hint of confidence. To this day, I don't know if

90

I took a wrong turn or if I just had gotten baptized into the frontier way of life. Looking back on that little adventure, the only thing I would like to experience again was that cute accent.

I sent a postcard or called at the end of each day. My next stop was Saskatoon, Saskatchewan, where I hit a horrible snowstorm. It was a whiteout! I could barely see in front of me. I pulled in the first chance I got. I didn't have my snow tires on yet, and I wanted to be safe until I did.

The place that I stayed at was a seasonal campground, closed for the winter. However, it had a few cabins and a small lodge. The lodge was open and served sandwiches and had a bar attached that had a pool table. Because it was pretty early when I checked in, I put my quarter up on the pool table and challenged the winner. The time passed quickly while I won a few games.

I learned that on a clear day I would be able to see Blackstrap Mountain in full view. Actually this was just a ski hill. Blackstrap Provincial Mountain is a provincial park with a manmade lake and campground. The so-called mountain was built for the Canada Winter Games and was the attraction of the area. I had seen Mount McKinley, so I wasn't impressed. There were several people who told me they were looking forward to skiing Blackstrap. There wasn't any TV reception in my little cabin, so I played pool until the lodge closed around 10:00 p.m.

Morning came sooner than I thought, even after going to bed so early. These cabins had no water piped into them, no shower, only a jug of water set inside the door. If I needed the bathroom, I'd have to go to the lodge.

The next morning, I took my overnight case and climbed into my truck, then drove off. I stopped at the first gas station I came to. With snow-covered ground and roads being plowed, I decided it was finally time to get the snow tires put on. Blackstrap was out in full view and was quite nice to see, exactly as the patrons at the lodge assured me the night before. But it was no Mount McKinley.

I had to wait to have the tires changed. When the man at the gas station asked how much air I wanted in them, I had no clue how to answer him. I hadn't been educated on what I needed to know. The attendant didn't have much patience waiting for my answer, as he had several people waiting for service.

I replied, "What do you suggest?" He was very abrupt and said, "Well, what's it going to be? 30....40.....50......60 pounds or what?"

I fumbled around, uhhing and errring, and was very frustrated not knowing what to answer. So I said, "Put in 60 pounds." I figured the more air, the farther I could go without having to check them again.

I filled up with those imperial gallons, 4.55 liters each, so much bigger than American gallons at 3.78 liters. I had the oil checked, paid for the service and off I went once again.

I was driving on snow-covered roads with my half-ton Chevy loaded down to the point that the rear end was hanging way down. Even in this short time in Canada, I was tickled with the Canadians' accent and how they answered many questions with sentences ending in "Eh." So cute and catchy.

The temperature was dropping to below freezing at night but stayed above 32 during the day.

The roads and skies were soon clear. The heat of the day melted away most of the snow on the road. The speed limits were 70 miles an hour. This was unheard of in Wisconsin where it was only 55. Even though I thought about making better time because the scenery was nothing but grain sheds and fields for miles, I stayed at about 50-55 mph.

Driving a loaded truck was a lot different than driving my convertible with its big engine. I was told that this type of truck would be economical to drive to Alaska and bring a nice profit if I sold it. It wasn't a flashy truck by any means. Actually, it was a horrible green color and kind of dull. It wasn't my choice of color, but what do men care about? All they cared about was what was under the hood.

My next destination was Edmonton, Alberta. It was full of many one-way streets. I kept getting turned around while trying to look at the map, the streets, the road signs and streetlights, all at the same time. I sure had to put my driving skills to work but I wasn't always successful.

I pulled in the circular driveway of a huge hotel at the city centre. The billboard featured a "Welcome" to some convention taking place there during my stay. I found a parking spot with a plug-in, plugged in my truck, checked in, found my room and dropped off my bag. I thought this might be a place to have a little fun. Nobody knew me or my name, so what did I care? Then I proceeded to freshen up a little, grabbed my accordion and found the convention ballroom. After peeking in, I realized this was a formal event.

I still planned on having a little fun. I strapped on my squeezebox and promenaded through the ballroom with about 400 people sitting down to dinner. I had them all clapping to the music by the time I made my way completely through the room. After I finished, I quickly exited the room and made my way to the nearest ladies room. There I let down my hair, brushed it out, took off my old red flannel shirt, wrapped my accordion in it, and went to the lounge off the ballroom. There I enjoyed a very good old-fashioned.

As I sipped my drink, two fellows dressed in tuxedos came in the bar talking about the entertainment. They laughed back and forth, trying to figure out whose brainstorm it was; that polka music was the highlight of their dinner. They mentioned no one knew anything about it. I sat there enjoying the moment, my accordion at my feet covered by my red shirt, knowing that I had gotten away with it. All free spirit, good fun. It was great, and I

The Alaska Highway

The Alaska Highway is one of the engineering wonders of the modern world. Its starting point is Mile 0 in Dawson Creek, British Columbia, Canada, and it ends in Delta Junction, Alaska, Mile 1523. Here it joins the Richardson Highway that connects Delta Junction to Fairbanks, the largest city in Interior Alaska. Some people miss the last milepost in Delta Junction and think they are on the Alaska Highway all the way to Fairbanks.

President Franklin D. Roosevelt authorized the construction of the Alaska Highway on February 6, 1942. Work began five days later with the understanding that the United States would cover the full cost and the finished road and other facilities in Canada would be turned over to Canadian authorities after the war ended. More than 16,000 civilians worked on the job. The total cost of the project was more than $138 million.

Although it was completed on October 28, 1942, the highway was not usable for vehicles until 1943. There were few guard rails, many steep grades, poor surfaces and many problem hills. Log bridges were built and later were replaced with steel ones.

In 1948 the Alaska Highway was opened to the general public, attracting vacationers and homesteaders.

Looking at the countryside, it was hard to imagine that in the early 1940s, this was all wilderness. One of the biggest problems was building on permafrost and muskeg ground. The inexperienced engineers didn't know what they were getting into. There was no limit on the money needed for the equipment and supplies to get the job done.

As I traveled this 1,200-mile gravel highway (only one percent was blacktopped), I felt I was truly a pioneer ready for any challenge ahead. What an opportunity this was to experience and travel the historic Alaska Highway.

had all could do not to giggle as they spoke. Eh!

I got up early the next day. It was cloudy and cold. I had breakfast and then went out and started my truck and let it run awhile to warm up. I have to say this little truck had a very warm heater in it. It was very comfortable. I was sure that no one would believe that I made it this far. I felt like a pioneer. I knew a lot of my friends and family thought I had a screw loose. Some probably thought I should have been committed, as they thought I lost my mind. *Why in the world would I want to go to a God-forsaken place with nothing but ice and snow?* is what a lot of people asked before I left.

My next destination was Dawson Creek, British Columbia. After the routine of having a little breakfast and gassing up, I was on my way. The cloudy skies turned sunny and crisp clean air and beautiful scenery was abundant for miles. When I reached Dawson Creek, I found the city centre and the Milepost Monument displaying the beginning of the Alaska Highway. The milepost shows distances from Dawson Creek to many major cities all over the world. (This is a must-stop to see if you should ever travel through the town.) It wasn't far to Fort St. John from here, my next destination.

About 10 miles south of Fort St. John, the plows had just completed their work ahead of me and I took a corner too close. The shoulder *looked* solid, but I was sucked into the ditch and hit a culvert.

Uh oh! CR-R-RASH!!

The damage was quite extensive. The frame was bent on my brand new truck and there was other damage I couldn't even begin to figure out. By now I only had about 2,500 miles on it. This was not going well.

Trying repeatedly to get out of the ditch, I stopped when I smelled something burning. I thought maybe my tires were getting too hot from spinning around.

When the tow truck arrived, the driver had a hard time getting my truck out of that hole. I guess all the stuff in back had thrown the cap off center.

Someone would have to reset it.

The guys back at the garage could see that this was a new truck. Because of this, they let me know that I would have to plan on waiting for parts and repairs. They parked the truck in an impound yard until it could be moved into the garage for the repairs. Because the back was so heavily loaded down, the guys wondered what the heck I had in there.

"All my worldly possessions," I replied, "I'm moving to Alaska!"

The body shop soon let me know that I would have to plan on staying in Fort St. John as all the parts had to be air-freighted in and that would take time.

Jim Kline was the station owner and tow truck manager. He was tall, lean and soft spoken, with a smile that would win an Oscar. I felt very lucky to have him oversee the decisions to be made. He let me know it was going to be impossible to get a room. Apparently, there were about 4,000 men in town for the yearly "bonspiel." I, of course, did not have a clue what he was talking about. Important questions started pouring out. "What am I to do for a room?" "What is a bonspiel?" "How long should I plan on being there?" "How far is it to the garage?"

Jim made a few calls but, as he thought, no rooms were available. He then offered me what he called an emergency workingman's room. Nothing fancy, of course, but set aside by the gas station at the Fort Motor Lodge for emergency cases. These rooms were used mostly by men, contracted to come into town, for as-needed jobs such as snow removal.

I was lucky there was such an option. It was clean, with a twin bed but no TV. It did have a bathroom but there was no tub, only a shower. There was no telephone or room service. Housekeeping was twice a week or as needed. In a way, this was great. It was easy walking distance to the station, garage and local businesses. This was in a grand old hotel with beautiful woodwork, custom carpeting in the lobby and great artwork covering the walls. As I checked in, I noticed all the pigeon hole mail slots for each room. I was comparing it to the fancy room I had in Edmonton. It was like walking back in time. NEAT!

Later in the day, I walked back to the gas station, about six blocks away, to find out what all this was going to cost. I had given them a few hours to determine what would be needed. That station would do the repairs under the hood, and then the garage would do the bodywork. Jim let me know right off the bat that I needed a new clutch because mine was burned out. He told me that he couldn't figure out how that could happen with such low mileage on the truck and suggested I call the dealer because it could be covered by the warranty. That could save me some money.

So, of course, I called Art right away.

Tina Tames the Town

Although I hadn't been gone for even a full week yet, Art wasn't at all surprised to hear my voice. Before I gave him the repair news, I asked him if he missed me. He said yes, so then I asked him, "How much?" He said, "A lot!" That made me feel better. I knew he would have loved to hear that I wanted to come straight home.

I told him that I had been in a wreck, but I didn't get hurt or hurt anyone. I also said I needed him to send me a clutch. He said "What? That's impossible," and that I didn't have enough miles on the truck to have that happen. He said that I must be mistaken and it must be some other part I needed. Rather than talk about what part it could be, I just put Jim on the line to confirm it.

As they talked, I realized that this being a brand new, off-the-showroom-floor vehicle, most of the parts needed for repairs would have to be ordered. After Jim talked to Art, he gave me back the phone. Art told me that the clutch had to be defective and he would see to it that I got a replacement covered by the warranty. Whether or not it was my fault, I knew Art had connections and would take care of it.

I pulled out all the boxes I wanted to take to the hotel room. The guys had emptied my truck and stored the contents, knowing the truck was going to be there awhile. Jim had one of his employees bring my instruments to my little room along with what I needed to maintain myself for the next 10 days or so. That made me feel good and it was very thoughtful.

After talking to Art, I called Paul and my mother to give them the news. I used the phone at the station and called each of them collect. I let them know I was going to be here for a while and promised I would let them know when I would be leaving. Until then, I would not be calling, as it was too expensive. I assured them I would send postcards.

This was going to be a more expensive trip than I had planned. There were pay phones in the lobby of the hotel if I wanted to call from there. The desk clerk told me to expect to pay a dollar a minute to call Wisconsin from the pay phone, just like in Alaska. Now that all my calls were made and Art would order my clutch, it was time for, what else? Cocktails! Walking back to the hotel, I was looking forward to enjoying a quiet drink in a beautiful lounge while listening to soft country music.

As I scooted up to the bar, I introduced myself to the bartender who let me know he was the regular bartender and that his name was Dez. He also said that he couldn't serve me unless I had a male escort. I thought he was kidding! No, he wasn't. After a bit, he got someone to be my "escort" for one drink. Apparently, this is truly a law in Canada, subjecting one to a severe fine if violated.

During my conversations with Dez, I mentioned I'd be happy to entertain his patrons with music if he would allow me to stay in the bar for a bit. He thought that was a great plan for both of us. I got the instruments, then played music and had all I could drink. He got a lot more business than usual and we both did well in tips.

Playing my favorite country songs was a big hit in the lounge. I acquired a new fan from Nova Scotia. His name was Mike, and he asked me to play *Don't Be Angry*, apparently his favorite. I didn't know the song, but I told him I could play anything he could sing. So off we went, him singing and me playing the accordion. What a great

song and from that day it became my favorite as well. This
night ended too soon, no matter what time that was.

The next morning promised to be very interesting. I
went down to the dining room only to find dozens of
people waiting for a table. This situation was due to the
bonspiel being held in town. I had never heard of this
competition and had no clue what this sport was. There
were MEN all over the place, and then some. Men-men-
men. All ages, all sizes, all right!

They were all very courteous, and I was able to go up
to the front of the line. The maitre d' asked if I minded
sharing a table with another young lady if she agreed
to my company. She was already seated and had her
coffee when he asked if she minded if I joined her. He
motioned me in, and I thanked her for letting me join her.
I introduced myself, as did she. Her name was Tina and
she was from Edmonton. She was a natural beauty.

She was very pleasant and sympathized with my
situation. After hearing my story, she let me know that
she, too, was going to be in town for at least a week
because of the bonspiel. She said she was an entertainer
also and would be performing at the cabaret across the
street from the hotel starting tonight. She invited me to see
her performance at 8:30. I thought that was very nice of
her. Being stranded in Fort St. John was getting better and
better.

After breakfast, I wanted to find out what this
"bonspiel" was all about. The desk clerk told me how to
get to where it was being held. It wasn't far, and I had to
walk right past the station where my truck was parked. I
stopped in to let them know where I was headed. Jim and
one of his buddies decided to join me.

As we walked over, Jim gave me a brief breakdown of
what curling was. Even with his explanation, it still was
a new experience to see it. The building was like walking
into an indoor ice skating rink. The guys were dressed
warm for the temperature. They each had a big rocklike

Tina   me

Tina and I partied all week long.

object with a handle protruding from the top. They would grip the handle and fling this rock down a lane of ice, similar to a bowling alley, and try to get as close to the target on the other end as possible. After one team member thrusts the rock, the other team members follow the stone down the lane and, with little brooms, sweep the ice vigorously, allowing the rock to move quickly or not, depending on their brushing technique. I didn't get a good look at the shoes these players were wearing, but I would imagine they were special, like you would need to glide when necessary.   At times the rock would knock other opponents rocks, similar to knocking over bowling pins to make points. The team that ends up closest to the target at the end of the lane wins.

Curling reminded me of growing up in an Italian neighborhood, watching the men play bocce ball every Sunday afternoon on the playground of the school. I left the building, with a big smile on my face. I was still smiling when I stopped back to the gas station. Noticing my happy face, Jim asked me what was so funny. I said that this sport simply intrigued me and I wondered if the American men could move just half as fast to sweep a driveway. I knew I would have to go back and watch this competition again.

It was now lunchtime. After a bite to eat, I walked around, bought a few postcards, wrote to everybody, stamped the cards, brought them to the desk clerk to be mailed and then checked out a few more places within walking distance. I quickly noticed that there was a large sales tax on everything I bought. I thought Wisconsin was high. Later, I found out that Canadians had a full health care plan paid for by these taxes.

When 8:00 p.m. rolled around, I started over to the cabaret. There was a doorman collecting cover charge money. I had no problem with that, but did have a problem getting in even though Tina invited me. Up popped that stupid law again. I needed a male escort. As I left, I thought about whom I could ask to get me in and see Tina.

Back to the station again. I told the guys I had an invitation to see my new friend Tina perform at 8:30 p.m. and that I couldn't get in without an escort. Boy, was I surprised when TWO of them offered to get me in. Then they called Jim to join us. All the guys were so anxious to be of help. I found that very refreshing. The men in Milwaukee were just the opposite. With 10 girls to every man there, they were pretty controlling. Girls in Milwaukee, in many cases, even paid their way on a date. Not me!

Another law they have in a cabaret is that food must accompany any drinks being served. There were snack menus on every table. By the time the drinks and food were served, Jim and two more guys arrived. About the time they sat down, the lights dimmed and the entertainment began.

A comedian came out first and told a few jokes that were actually pretty funny. Then an announcer waved his arms, the music started, lights started flashing and out comes this gal dressed like Cleopatra. She was draped in all kinds of silk scarves and long, long black hair. As she walked around the stage, black lights were turned on and cans of florescent paint were placed in a row on the front of the stage.

She would take off one of the scarves, which left a little bit of skin showing, and looped it over one of the audience guys and pulled him on stage. He was then part of her act. He had to pick a color and take the paintbrush and paint the bare spot on her body that was left when she removed the scarf she had used to loop him up on stage. The music kept going as she kept lassoing guys on stage until all the scarves were gone and all the bare skin was painted. By the final part of the performance, her entire body was fully painted and looked snakelike as she promenaded around the stage totally naked.

As she made her final pass around the stage, she leaned over to me and asked how I liked her dance. I was stunned. She looked nothing like the woman I had breakfast with this morning. No wonder the guys were so eager to be my escorts—she was a nude dancer! I have to admit, however, it was done in very good taste. After the entertainment, the lights came up and Tina came out and told us not to leave. She said she had to shower off all the paint and change and would be back soon.

Most of the crowd left after the show, but those that stayed moved to tables closer to the bar and introduced themselves. I had several ask me if I was visiting someone in Fort St. John and a few thought I was with Tina. I let everyone know that I was passing through and waiting for my truck to be repaired. As they were checking me out, I was doing the same with them. I was enjoying the conversation, all the guys and, of course, all the free drinks.

While waiting for Tina, I felt like the belle of the evening. Before Tina got back, I let everyone know I was a musician, played the squeezebox and could play just about anything they could sing. By this time, Tina had returned and, of course, all the attention switched to her. That was fine. I knew there would be lots of fun ahead with her on my side. She and I laughed at how naïve' I was about this business of hers.

She was an artist and a professional at what she did. Even though she ended up stark naked, the black light neon paints covered her whole body and the finale of her act was elegant. Watching a dancer (I hate to say stripper) for the first time, which I never would have gone out of my way to see, was enjoyable. The guys had a lot of fun teasing me about the whole event. Now I know why they were more than happy to be my escorts.

When it was closing time, the owner locked all the doors. The bartenders came out from behind the bar and joined us with jokes and more laughs.

Parties were going on all throughout the town. Many of them were in places like the one I was at and many others were in hospitality rooms of the motels and hotels where the bonspiel participants were staying. Apparently some of these guys had invited Tina to their parties and, now that we were friends, she invited me to go along. She told me to bring my squeezebox for added fun. She said that there was a lot of money floating around and that there might be a lot of tips in it for both of us.

We planned on taking in as many of these parties as we could during this tournament. This party night however, was going to stay in-house. We were having a great time making new friends with the cabaret staff, owners, Jim, the Esquires' band members and all my escorts. As we got to know everyone's name, we could see friendships forming. We finally called it a night and walked across the street to our hotel. We both had certain guys we were attracted to, but neither of us had any intentions of rushing into

Jim Kline

Jim and me at the cabaret.

anything. We just laughed about our favorites all the way home. Tomorrow was another day. We agreed to meet for breakfast at 11:00 a.m. Not too early, as it was already almost morning.

I was glad that I was able to sleep in. No need to get up early and hit the road. It seemed as though I just laid my head on the pillow when one of Jim's staff was pounding on my door. I was wanted at the station for some signatures to authorize the work to be done. I asked if I could do it later and was advised Jim was waiting for my "John Hancock" so he could have my truck moved to the garage that was going to do the work. Even though the parts hadn't arrived, it seemed pretty important.

I was down there at the station, without my coffee, within half an hour. When I got there, everyone got a good laugh, as it was just a joke. I was offered coffee, but they didn't have real cream, just that powdered stuff. My coffee of choice was with sugar and cream. I just couldn't deal with Coffee-Mate or any other powdered creamer. I had my coffee with a little sugar. It was not the same.

When I got back to the hotel, Tina was waiting. She was her gorgeous self. She had the most beautiful complexion and wore very little make-up. I felt special to be her friend. I had my coffee of choice (with real milk or cream) as we waited for our breakfast and talked about the night before, all the laughs and people we met.

Now we were deciding on which party to attend after her performance. I told her I would be at her show again. I knew I would have no problem getting an escort. The guys at the station were ready to go. I had my cards to write and sleep to catch up on, so we made plans for the evening and went our separate ways until then. I wrote my cards, then gave them to the desk clerk to mail and took a nap.

By the time I got up, it was suppertime, and then time to enjoy a cocktail with Dez in the lounge. I left my accordion there the night before. I thought about my new admirer from Nova Scotia. Sure enough, he was there waiting for me. He had some friends with him and introduced them to me. Their cute little accents just intrigued me all the more. Eh! When nine o'clock rolled around, I announced that I had planned on going across the street to the cabaret. It seemed that the news of Tina's performance had spread through the town.

When I hit the door, even though I had followers, the doorman was instructed to let me in solo. That was cool. I made my way to the table I was at the night before to find the whole gang already there. My fans from the hotel sat nearby. The place was packed. The band sounded pretty good and everyone seemed to be having a good time. I noticed a change at the bar. Last night's bartender, Alex, was now seated at our table.

He wanted to introduce me to Dennis, a little person, who was making drinks like crazy. Booze bottles were flying. The waitresses were very busy calling off the drinks. A ramp was behind the bar, raising the floor level for Dennis. Dennis was now at the same height Alex had been without the ramp. He was very confident and good at his job. You could see that he really liked women. The evening had pretty much the same routine as the pleasurable night before. When Tina joined us after her act, we all made plans to take in one of the parties nearby.

The hospitality room was going great by the time we all got there. Food and drinks were plentiful. There were mostly guys there and they were happy to see us. I had brought my squeezebox and everyone was eager to hear the music.

I played anything they could sing. They loved mostly country. Thanks to my past with my first boyfriend, Bobby Ray Hoover, I had learned several hundred country songs from his musical friends. I was a big hit. As the evening went on, the guys were tipping me especially good on the songs they requested. I made a bundle.

I lost track of Tina somewhere along the way, but that was ok. As the night went on, things slowed down in the wee hours. I decided to stay put and curled up on the couch. There were people sleeping in every possible corner. There was even a couple making love right on the floor in the middle of all of us. These two had just met for the first time that night. Her name was Jamie and his name was Ray. I made it a point to remember his name because he was my type of guy. I had my focus on him.

I was especially attracted to him because of his sense of humor and his ability to sing ALL the words to the songs I played. He also was the moneyman of the group and occasionally showed off his wad of multi-colored Canadian bills. The party people all had big money and said it was from oil development.

Eventually, the party died down and we all found a place to sleep. I didn't know about the rest of them, but the moans and groans of Ray and Jamie got my attention. I wanted to sleep but my attention was on them. They really went to it, not caring who heard them. Finally things were quiet.

When morning hit, I realized about a dozen of us had the same idea. We all looked at each other, fumbling around looking for something to cure our headaches and wondering who else heard the passion of the night.

After a few Bloody Mary's, we all went to the restaurant for coffee. No real milk or cream in the place. I had my coffee with sugar and focused on getting someone to drive me and my stuff back to the hotel. I put the accordion in the lounge for tonight and hit the hotel restaurant for some good coffee. I wrote my cards, dropped them off at the desk to be mailed and walked down to the gas station.

I decided to call Paul collect, which must have cost a bundle to Healy, Alaska. He accepted the charges, anxious to hear how far a got. I told him I had gotten into an accident and was now in Fort St. John, safe and sound. He told me that he called my mother to see if she heard from me. I said I mailed everyone cards each day, and I was waiting for parts. I really didn't want to hear his mush, but got through it. I told him to let my mother know that he had heard from me.

He was curious what I was doing to pass the time as I had no wheels and didn't rent a car. I told him I found the library and stopped in there from time to time, as it was within walking distance. I also checked out the nearby stores. That seemed to work for him for now.

After I hung up, I felt like a little kid having to answer for my whereabouts. That was something I didn't intend on making a habit. I also had to listen to the same opinion from him about the clutch. I replied, "I'm no mechanic!"

As I walked down to the gas station, I saw the garage manager talking to Jim. They decided to get my truck into the shop for some bodywork while waiting for parts. This would save some time. I agreed. After re-securing the camper shell cap, they pulled the truck over to the body shop.

The temperatures were getting colder. The bonspiel was still in full force. Lots of traffic and hustle-bustle in the area. As the first few days went pretty fast, I knew the next week wouldn't be moving so fast after the curling tournament came to an end and all the teams went back home. Most likely, so would my friend Tina. Her agent set her schedule and she had a full tour lined up.

Jim and all the guys let me know how impressed they were with my music and asked me to play after Tina's act back at the cabaret when we had our private party. That was fine with me. The guys loved to sing. They loved to get little Dennis going too, as I would find out.

By the time I got back to the hotel, the lounge was open. Cheese trays were served on the bar. No reason to have dinner with all this, I thought. Dez had already heard about our night of music and fun from his clientele. By this time, we became friends and teased each other back and forth. I loved it. Everybody so far was a good sport. It was a given that everyone was going over to the cabaret for Tina's performance.

This night, however, the guys had a special plan they cooked up for Dennis. They had gotten a hold of a letter he had written the night before. Apparently, it was sticking out of his back pocket while partying with us. It was still open and addressed to his cousin in Fort Nelson. Tina was supposed to perform in this town next. The letter read that Dennis lucked out with Tina! (We all had something to say about that.) They showed the letter to Tina, which ticked her off immensely. She agreed with the guys to teach this little charmer a lesson.

Alex was bartending, so the guys kept the drinks coming for Dennis. With him not knowing what was ahead, he was enjoying all the attention. Tina even added to the fun. She asked him to be sure and stick around for her return after her act. He was ecstatic that she even gave him the time of day. I knew something was up, but didn't know what.

Dennis was still going, drink after drink. He sure could pack em' in for a little guy. Tina struck up a conversation with Dennis. She asked him where he was from, etc. Then she asked him if he knew anyone in Fort Nelson, her next destination. He confirmed that he had a cousin there. She said she knew someone there, and named his cousin. Watching his face change in amazement, she held up the letter he wrote in front of his face, asked him how he could write such a thing, and wanted him to explain. He made all kinds of excuses, hemming and hawing. She listened while everyone waited until he fell asleep, passing out from all the booze. It didn't take long.

Now the guys kicked in their plan to cure him of being ungentlemanly. Dennis always wore one of those two-

The gang takes an inebriated Dennis out for his comeuppance.

110

inch-wide tooled western belts that had his name on the back. The buckle was a huge sterling silver oval. Four of the guys motioned to each other, got up at the same time and carried him out to the back of the cabaret where they had a heavy duty clothes line strung out. They took Dennis out there and ran that line under his belt and hung him out there by his backside. It didn't take long for him to come to.

His little arms and legs were swinging about and the language was horrible to hear coming from such a little guy. He fussed and threatened like a banty rooster. It was cold and he demanded to be let down. Tina came out at this point and asked for an apology and his promise never to do this type a thing again.

With his promise and apology, the guys finally took him down off the clothesline. After the dust settled, we all had a good laugh, called it a night and went on our way. What a night this was!

Tempted to Stay

The day that Jim told me the parts had come in should have been a happy day. A week had gone by. I should have been happy. By now, I 'd made a lot of friends and had more fun than I ever dreamed possible, with all the jokes and laughs.

Even though I had good insurance, the deductible ate up all my travel money. I knew I wouldn't have enough for the trip after I paid the rest. I had planned on calling Paul, who I had practically forgotten during this wonderful week in Fort St. John, to ask him for a loan. When I told Jim what my plan was, he could see that I would have a real hard time being indebted to Paul. He told me to figure out what I would need and that he would loan me the money. I could pay him back when I got a job.

I couldn't believe it, that someone I'd known only a week would be so kind. I let him know he would never regret it. He told me that I was one of the few people he knew that he could be sure to get his money back. The truck would soon be roadworthy. With my favorite fan at the hotel getting the word, he let me know how much he would miss me.

The next night when I stopped in the lounge, Dez let me know how sad Mike was and gave me a heads up that he had a gift for me. I played music as always, but tonight was different for Mike.

With his cute accent from Nova Scotia, he joined in. I

played the song he taught me, *Don't Be Angry*, which we called our song. He told me, whispering in my ear, that he had something for me. He had to let me know his feelings had grown for me and asked me to stay to give us some time. He was a real nice guy, and I seriously gave it some thought. I mulled around what I would have to do to stay. I didn't know what it would take, not being a citizen, to stay.

I wasn't thinking marriage, but I thought about staying. After weighing my options, I decided to follow my original plan. Mike and I had a nice discussion about the pros and cons. He let me know that he had gotten me a gift. When he pulled out a little black box from his pocket, knowing ahead of time what Dez told me, I felt pretty uncomfortable.

He then told me he had gotten me a silver coin with Queen Elizabeth on it, uncirculated and dated 1971. It was enclosed in its own blue velvet box and topped by clear plastic so each side could be seen. I told him I would cherish it forever, along with our song. Dez let me know later that he had another little black box in his other pocket; he was sure was a ring. He didn't pull it out when he realized I had my mind made up to continue my trip to Alaska. Needless to say, the tears streamed down my face uncontrollably. I hurt a very decent man, but I didn't want a close relationship ever again. I knew I would surely miss him and his cute accent.

Now it was time to deal with the gang. The bonspiel was ending and Tina was booked to go to another town soon. Everybody had to go back to his or her regular routine soon, which didn't include me. The timing would be about right as it was closing in on my departure day. I was still dropping a line daily, and sending a postcard to my mother, to let everyone know I was still in Fort St. John.

When I dropped my cards at the desk the Friday before I left, I was greeted by the Royal Canadian Mounted Police. The officer asked me if I wouldn't mind answering a few questions. I agreed while my thoughts went spinning. Was I in trouble for frequenting the lounge without an escort? Flirting with someone's husband? (I knew Jim was married and possibly Dez, and who knows who else.) Did we break the law when we hung Dennis out on the line? Did he file charges on all of us? What? What could this possibly be about?

He let me know that my mother had filed a missing persons report. In her report she claimed she hadn't heard from me since the day I arrived in Fort St. John. I told him that this couldn't be, as I faithfully sent her a card every day. He noted all my answers for his report and as we were talking in the lobby, the desk clerk overheard our conversation.

The officer told me my mother was frantic, worried that I had driven over some cliff never to be found etc., etc. He encouraged me to call her as soon as possible. About that time, the desk clerk excused himself and interrupted. He let us both know that my cards had all been returned to my box at the hotel. I was puzzled as to how that could be. As he handed me all the cards, the officer watched.   They were returned because I used U.S. stamps to mail them! I had no clue I had to use Canadian stamps only.

Needless to say, I got to the nearest phone after I got about $10.00 in Canadian money, and called her. You could tell by her shaken voice how relieved she was to hear my voice. The stamp story, I'm sure, was hard for her to believe, and I was puzzled and stunned by that rule. I had never thought about checking the little box for me at the hotel because who would write to me here?

Now I had to call Paul with the same story, and of course Art. These were the hardest phone calls to make. This was unbelievable. In the states, the post office would just collect the postage due; this would have been no big deal. I never thought this little screw-up was cause enough for something as serious as having a missing persons report filed.

The policeman was glad his search had a happy ending. None of my cards mentioned the Fort Motor Hotel except one. That was where the search began. All of my other cards were of the area scenery and animals. By the time this confrontation was finished, everyone in the lounge, the desk clerk, and who knows whom else, knew the whole story. How could I have screwed up so badly? And here I thought I was being so responsible.

I had to shake the edge off, so I decided to wear my blonde wig, as blondes had more fun as the saying goes. Somehow I felt more feminine as a blonde. I got a lot of attention that night. I'd like to think it was the wig and not the fact that everyone knew I was leaving soon. Dennis was bartending, the band was playing and Tina was performing her last show. We were all sad, but reminiscing the good times.

Dennis had recovered from being hung out to dry. He felt really good that night, justified, I guess, because he thought I deserved a little care. For a little person, about four feet tall, he sure could dance and bartend. He was cute too. I could see how he could have charmed Tina into his arms. Dennis was ten feet tall in his own eyes.

On the Road Again

Waking up this morning, I was full of mixed emotions. I had my luggage packed and ready to take down to the lobby. It was very hard for me to leave. A part of me wanted to stay, and a part of me wanted to pursue my dream for a new life in the land of so-called ice and snow. Temperatures and daylight hours were dropping very quickly as each day passed. Today was cloudy, light snow and about 20°F.

I had a last breakfast with Tina and Jim. We said what we needed to say when friends part, enjoyed our breakfast and made our way to the gas station. The guys brought my truck around to the front when they spotted us coming. They were really having fun and laughing like crazy when they handed me the keys.

As I took that first look at my repaired truck, my eyes teared up again. The guys had taken the time and painted the names of every guy I had met in town all over my camper shell. Each letter of every name was painted in a different color. These names were plastered all the way around the shell. I couldn't help but feel all the time and love they had put into this project. The camper shell now had quite a rainbow color effect.

The truck was filled with gas and oil and all the fluids had been checked while I kissed and hugged all my friends that were there to see me off. I made sure that my snacks, thermos, camera, film and, of course, my precious trophy (the mounted doe head) were all up front with me.

Under the seat was a loaded pistol, and behind the front seat was my new 30-06 Remington rifle, still in the box. The pistol was somehow shoved up into the cushion padding, which had a specially made pouch in the padding. I had promised Bob never to tell anyone about it and only to use it if I got into serious trouble.

My thermos had black coffee in it, as I could not tolerate powdered creamers. This gal was from dairy country; she had to have real cream or milk or nothing for her coffee.

As I started the truck and made my way out of town, there was a lot of waving and whistling. The sun was still hiding. As I was driving through the main streets of Fort St. John, it wasn't long before a heard a siren behind me. Moving over to the curb, I was thinking an ambulance must have been coming through. Looking in my side mirrors, it now became apparent the siren was on a patrol car AFTER ME!!!

What had I done now? As I sat and waited I wondered. It turned out I was being stopped for running a red light. As I looked all over for it, the officer pointed it out hanging above the center of the intersection. *"How stupid was that?"* I was thinking, wondering if he could read my mind. As he wrote me the ticket, I noticed the address of the police station.

I got directions and immediately went to the station to pay the ticket and then my curiosity got the best of me. I paid the fine, no contest, because I wanted to get on my way. However, I needed to know why they wrote Fort St. John, B.C. The officer asked, what did I mean?

He told me it meant Fort Saint John, British Columbia. I chuckled as I turned and headed out the door. Then I turned back and said, "I thought B.C. meant Before Christ, having a stoplight placed where no one would see it." *Like caveman mentality, no common sense,* I silently mumbled as I walked to my truck. I had to get back to my departure on the highway north to Alaska.

It took a lot for me to refocus my thoughts while crying. It was about noon when I actually left and only a few miles before I was back on gravel roads. It felt good to be behind the wheel on my way to *Alaska*! I called Art, my mother, and Paul to let them know I was back on the road again.

After a bit, I felt my pioneer spirit taking over again. It helped to be wearing all my traveling gear, particularly my Red Wing boots and wool socks that reached almost up to my knees. I knew the temperature had dropped, but I passed on putting on the long johns. I had on a long-sleeved turtleneck top, jeans, a heavyweight red plaid shirt, and a little red hat that I had worn when I had gone hunting.

I felt carefree and wanted to take my time, enjoy everything and see all that I could see. I drove down the middle of the road; I thought I should be a little more cautious on this leg of the trip. The roads had not yet been plowed clear of the snowfall just hours before. I could easily follow the worn roadway ruts. Traffic was ok and I felt comfortable behind the wheel. I was sure everything that had needed to be checked or fixed had been expertly done back in Fort St. John. It was an overwhelming relief not to have to answer to anyone.

Things were going fine as darkness started to set in. I had to use headlights even though things were still visible. The snow flurries started up again and finally daylight disappeared.

Driving now made me more attentive, and it wasn't even late yet. The roads were only two lanes wide. Then I saw the vehicle ahead of me losing control. It wasn't going very fast, but still, the driver could not keep his truck on the road. He slid softly into the ditch on the opposite side of the road, front bumper first.

I had enough time to slow down and tried to help. There were no buildings or traffic now, so I thought I should stop and see if anyone had been hurt. I knew that was the right thing to do. Little did I know that when I got closer and applied my breaks, I too would slide into the very same hole. Was I mad!

I tried to get out. The harder I tried, the deeper I sunk. That stick-shifting was for the birds. Frustrated, to put it mildly, I got out of my truck and made it up to the road. The people in the other vehicle were not hurt either and were also ticked off. The highway patrol was right on the spot and radioed back to Jim's Garage in Fort St. John for a tow truck. We were at Trutches Crossing.

The guys at Jim's would have to come about 100 miles or so to get me. Getting antsy while waiting for help to arrive, I tried to back my truck out over and over to no avail. It seemed a lifetime passed until they got there. When the tow truck door opened and I saw an ear-to-ear smile and that long-legged tall guy stepping out of the cab, I was overjoyed. It was Jim!

He came out himself with one of the guys in another truck to tow the other party. I jumped into his truck as they hooked up the rigs. Jim let me know that when I got back to town, I might have to call Art again. I wondered why? He said I might have to have order some more parts. I couldn't imagine why. But whatever Jim said was fine with me.

As we drove back to town, I told Jim about my ticket, from which he got a laugh. We talked more about how the truck handled after the repairs and Tina's next performance, where she was headed next, and when. Before I knew it, we were pulling into Fort St. John. His other truck was right behind us. We passed his station with my truck still a tow, while his other truck pulled into the station. I just thought Jim was going to make another sweep and come around to enter his compound behind his other driver. That was not the plan at all.

He pulled up to the Fort St. John Hotel and opened the front door for me. All my friends had gathered in the lounge. Dez and friends had taken up a collection and raised enough money to help me with my expenses. I was looking at another week, at least, if parts had to be ordered. There was about $300.00 in the collection. I was amazed. How great were these friends!

Tina got the cabaret to extend her booking here another week, even though the bonspiel was over and all the participants were on their way home. She had acquired quite a local following and could justify it to her agent, even though the curlers were gone. I got my same little emergency workingman's room back at the hotel. I thought I would wait until tomorrow to make any needed phone calls.

I was overwhelmed at the generous gestures of time, money, courtesy and friends greeting me on my return. I didn't give Alaska much thought at this point.

We all finished our drinks and made our way across the street to the cabaret. Even though Tina was not on the program, all of us, including her, enjoyed the music. We all laughed as we explained why I was still there. We were starving and this time I was glad to order food with my drink. Alex was bartending and it wasn't long before Dennis popped in. The Jim hotline was very efficient. Jim's lovely wife also came. We had never met before, but we each had heard a lot about the other. She was a very good sport. Jim was always the perfect gentleman, and I let her know that. She had no doubts.

Even though I had a great homecoming, in a way, all of us were pretty partied out after a hard week of giving it our best. Everyone was happy when we all dispersed early, about 10:30 p.m. Tomorrow would be another day.

Déjà vu'

There is something to the old adage, "early to bed, early to rise." I woke up at 6:30 the next morning. It was way too early to do anything. I took a shower, fixed my hair the best I could without resorting to putting on my wig, got dressed and went down to the restaurant for breakfast.

It was too early even for breakfast, so I started with coffee. I knew it would be awhile before Tina would be down. I got the newspaper, read the news, and tried to do the crossword while passing the time. I finally felt like a bite to eat and ordered a little breakfast. It wasn't long before Tina came in. We reviewed what happened the day before and agreed it was meant to be. I really didn't want to leave Fort St. John just yet.

I told Tina I hadn't made any calls to my mother, Art and Paul, and how much I was dreading them. It was times like this that I felt like a little kid. But, a promise is a promise. Not quite ready for that part of my day, I sat with Tina a while longer and had more coffee. We decided to walk down to the gas station to see what we could find out. It was about 9:00 and the guys had already gone through the truck inside and out.

Jim was in the garage and came out to let us know what the situation was. The good news was there was no body damage, but the bad news was I had burned out another clutch.

I asked, "How could that be? How could that happen?

I only drove about a hundred miles."

Jim had no answers.

Oh well, now I had more to add to my conversation when I make my calls. That meant another clutch had to be ordered. I wondered what kind of truck Art sold me. Was I going to have to deal with this problem all along the way to Alaska? Jim thought I should call Art first so he could confirm the trouble. When I finally got Art on the phone to tell him I needed another clutch, he couldn't believe it. I told him, "What about me? I can't believe it either."

Here I was, only halfway to Alaska, already been in an accident and somehow burned out *two* clutches. Delayed about eight days so far, I was going to be here at least another week. Art told me he would have to get approval to get one shipped to us ASAP. He just had to figure out what to tell them to get the approval. I was to call him back in about an hour. Before he hung up, however, he had to try and get me to admit I ruined it or find out what I had done to burn it out.

He said it was almost impossible for this to happen—unless I was doing something wrong. He made me tell him, step by step, everything that happened while driving this stretch of the road and while I got towed back to Fort St. John. As I was carefully telling him what I could remember, he surmised I was "riding the clutch." He kept repeating the phrase, "You must have been riding the clutch." That got to be really annoying and I finally lashed back at him.

I said, "So where IS the damn clutch?" I sure had no clue. He let me know it was the other pedal, next to the brake pedal. Oh, *that* pedal.

"What do you mean, 'riding the clutch?'" He said, "You must have had your foot on it hard enough to depress it as you were driving. Were you doing that?" he asked.

I gave it some thought and replied, "So that's where the clutch is. I thought that pedal was a FOOT REST."

Now that the whole story was told, Art finally knew what he was dealing with. Me too! I would have to watch my lead foot while driving. I told him I would call him back in about an hour.

I called my mother to let her know what happened. Her reply was, "That's enough. Get back home *now*. You can still save your job. Don't be crazy." I told her not to worry for about a week, as I 'm not doing anything until the clutch was replaced.

My next call was to Paul up in Alaska. He said, "You gotta be kidding. Nobody burns out a clutch in a hundred miles." I let him know right then and there that I didn't appreciate being called a liar. He backed down right away. He apologized and asked if I needed money. I said "no" very firmly, thanked him and told him I would be here for at least another week. I reminded him this wasn't my plan either.

Now that I had those two calls out of the way, I called Art back. Somehow, he managed to order another clutch to be shipped to Canada. No charge. Jim couldn't believe it. He commented, "No wonder he sells so many vehicles. He sure gets things done."

Art worked for Braeger Chevrolet in Milwaukee. He was the top salesman of the year. Vicki, the gal that introduced us, let me know this to impress me. This all had been a stressful few hours. Now that everything was taken care of, for the moment anyway, it was lunchtime. Actually way past lunchtime. It was about 2:00 p.m. by now. I went back to the hotel to let Tina know what the latest news was.

We decided to walk around the area and see if there was more to Fort St. John than what we had already found. We talked about the coming week and how we were going to spend our time. It was going to be another week of party time! I didn't think we would be able to top the week we just ended.

We went back down to the station. The guys had

pulled my truck out of the yard. The part would probably be here in about three days. Exactly when the part arrived and how the jobs ahead of mine went would determine when I could plan on leaving for the second time. In any case, we had at least five days before I could depart again.

As we entered the hotel that afternoon, the day shift employees were surprised to see me again and wondered what had happened. As I explained the whole story once again, we all had another nice reunion. I have to say, it is pretty nice to be greeted by name when you walk into an establishment. That night we were invited to have dinner at the home of one of the girls who worked at the cabaret. Her name was Eleanor and she was a hostess there. We got there about 6:30 to find Dennis already there. It was kind of nice to be in a house environment again. Even though I hadn't been gone that long from my apartment, I missed it.

The rest of the gang rolled in and some of the guys brought their girlfriends or wives. The week before, the guys had still been on the clock. That night, Jim let them all have a little fun. They all worked at figuring out and swapping work hours. Someone would be at the station during regular open hours, but everyone would still have a chance to enjoy the party.

All the girls were great, and some of them even brought a hot dish to share. Some of the guys even brought a bottle. Before you knew it, we were dancing and singing. Dennis was going to town. He got to dance with everybody. Tina was definitely his favorite. She was OK with that and the rest of us enjoyed the entertainment.

After just a week in Fort St. John, I didn't miss my former city life at all. The days passed pretty quickly while waiting for the clutch. Before I knew it, the clutch was here and Jim made sure my truck was brought in the shop as soon as it arrived. My clutch was replaced in no time, and I was ready to be on my way again. I had the same kind of send off, if not even more fun, the second time.

Now the guys at the station were teasing me. They were making bets that I would be back. I was even going to bet on that myself!

As I pulled away from my friends for the second time, I focused on getting on the road again with no distractions. Low and behold, I made it all the way to Fort Nelson, 240 miles with no problems. I passed Trutches Crossing with caution and a smile. I gathered my confidence once again.

Fort Nelson was a good-sized town and an easy place to find lodging. As I entered the lodges and hotels throughout Canada, it seemed that country music was playing everywhere. That was fine with me. I knew most of the songs, if not the words, and I could play them anyway because of the melodies. Many country songs are based on similar melodies.

As the evening came about, so did the music. I didn't know what the rules were in this part of Canada regarding having an escort, but made the same deal with the hotel manager to play music as I did in Fort St. John. It was a very pleasant evening that I would look forward to remembering after I called it a night.

Northern Lights and Happy Nights

Today I had no problems other than finding a place to fill up with gas. My reference book, the 1971 forest green *Alaska Milepost* I depended on, let me know what to expect ahead. I had traveled far enough to reach the red line on the gas gauge. I didn't get too nervous, even though the last three businesses were all closed up for the season. In this part of the world, things were pretty isolated and traffic was very infrequent.

I knew my little half-ton pick-up was very good on gas, so I assumed I had about 25 miles before I would really be in trouble. Looking back, I never thought I would reach the point of being stranded. It never sank in that I could get in serious trouble in an instant. Since I had a very good heater in the truck, I never thought about the temperature being about -30° F right outside my windows with the gas gauge almost on empty. The book said the next stop was about *50 miles* (or 80 kilometers) away.

After evaluating my approximate gas, mileage and the frigid temperature outside, I finally realized with a sinking feeling that I was in trouble again. *Big trouble.* I wasn't going to make it to a gas station in time!

Think! Think! Your life depends on this!

I decided I had better stop anyone passing by. If I saw a vehicle coming, I would jump out and put the hood up.

I did that twice and got passed up both times! I can't believe this is happening! *Don't panic.*

Finally I heard someone else coming. By now I was getting real nervous, not to mention cold. Would this be my last chance? *Don't sit there. Do something!* Quickly, I jumped out after I turned off the truck and put the hood up. This time it was a huge double-tanker semi. The driver was surprised I was traveling alone and didn't realize how many businesses had totally shut down, not to mention completely vacated during the winter months. He also thought this wonderful *Milepost* book should give stronger warnings to winter travelers.

The tanker was hauling fuel that had to be mixed somehow to make gasoline. He had enough to fill up a gas station. Maybe several gas stations! *Saved.* The driver made a makeshift funnel out of a plastic gallon jug to mix fuel from his two tankers, then filled my gas can four times with these makeshift gas mixtures. During this whole ordeal, I ran totally out of gas while waiting for help.

These truck tankers had nozzles the size of the ones on fire hoses. He had no adapter to downsize the tap, so this process was quite a long ordeal. It was a lot of work, especially in the cold. The cap had to be opened just enough to cause a drip mode that would compare to the force of a household water hose. Then he had to fill half of the gallon jug from one tanker, seal the tap, go to the other tanker, fill the jug with the other half of fuel to make the gas, and then put it in my tank.

After he filled my truck, I followed him to the next open roadhouse called the Fireside Inn at Mile 543. After all that and being chilled to the bone, I was more than determined to call this a day. I rented a room and went to the lounge, which was also the poolroom, restaurant and gift shop. I bought the driver dinner for helping me. He was so nice, I almost had to force him to let me do it.

As we ate together enjoying a nice supper, I forgot to get his name. The folks at the inn seemed to know him, so I felt comfortable. We both had fish and chips served with malt vinegar. That was a first for me. It's a Canadian or English additive to deep fried fish. After we finished dinner, the waitress hinted that she wanted to clear the table so that she could close out her shift. Then we went up the bar.

The first few drinks were on him. I suggested we shoot pool for the next rounds. I love to shoot pool. The tougher the opponent, the better I like it. I was very cautious about how badly to beat him. He was good and not that easy to beat. He then wanted to call it a night, as he had to get an early start the next morning.

I thought he had checked in at the inn, but when I saw him headed to the front door, I asked him if he needed help bringing anything in. He explained he was sleeping in his truck, which he had left running outside. Then he pointed out a little extension off the rear of the cab that was his bunk. I asked if I could take a peek, as this was another thing I had never seen. He hoisted me up to the cab and then joined me and showed me his sleeping quarters. It also had a hi-fi stereo unit, an ice cooler, a heater, magazines and even beer. This was all so compact and "cool."

He helped me down and walked me back to my room as we enjoyed watching the northern lights. It was the first time I had seen them. The sky was clear and the lights were awesome. I just couldn't believe how beautiful they were and how they danced all over the sky. The colors varied from blues and greens to whites and reds. It was so unbelievable.

When we got to my room, I invited him in. At this point he looked pretty good to me. Not thinking about tomorrow, we dropped everything (and I mean everything) and enjoyed the passion of the night. The northern lights were in full beauty and in full view through the window. I didn't think about anything but enjoying the moment and not worrying about who thought what. Fireworks of color burst across the skies outside, while fireworks were going off inside.

I fell asleep in total contentment, but when I awoke, my bed was empty. My white knight had jumped into his big semi and taken off. What a memory that was. I had hoped to see him somewhere up the highway, but I never saw him again. As I continued up the road, my thoughts finally burst; I finally realized what a horrible situation I could have experienced had it not been for him. I got a taste of what *real* cold could do to you. What I thought was being warmly dressed wouldn't have given me 30 minutes to live if I had ended up stranded and out of gas in the deadly cold.

Over the Edge

This morning, the temperature had dropped to –50°F or so in Fort Nelson. I had heard about this happening, but I never thought I would experience it so early in the trip. Nor could I anticipate what else would happen to me today. Apparently I was very lucky because my truck started at that temperature (plugged in, of course), but the locals advised me to stay put because of my inexperience driving in these conditions. I had several experienced male advisors in Fort St. John tell me the same thing while I was waiting for my truck parts.

Before taking off, I considered what people were telling me. Even though there was no wind, the temperature was piercing to the bone. It could sneak up on you before you knew it. I decided to try it for a few miles with a full tank of gas, a good truck heater, and all the fluids good. The road was gravel and plowed. As I went along, the thumping my tires caused subsided, and I gathered more and more confidence that I made the right decision.

I was warned that my tires would have a flat spot and that the rubber would have to warm up. The heat would round them out after driving awhile under these temperatures. This was amazing to me and would have been a concern had they not gone back to their regular shape.

The scenery was spectacular as I looked over the valley. The stands of trees were huge and covered the straight down drops following the cliffs on this section of the road.

As I drove along trying to get the feel of things, I wondered about the semi truck drivers mastering these narrow tight curves along sections of this road.

Everything was going along fine. I had traveled several miles when I heard several loud short noises sounding like a huge balloon popping. I quickly started swerving after the first pop, letting me know a tire blew. Then the others followed. Instantly, I completely lost control. I had no hope to keep the truck on the road. Things happened so fast, the last thing I remember was heading toward the edge. I remember hitting the plowed snow and surging so fast that the snow gushed up over my hood and blocked my windshield as I felt the truck thrashing downward. Then things went black.

I had no idea how long I had blacked out. All I know is that when I opened my eyes, it was blurry and when my eyes focused, two big brown eyes were looking back at me. For a second I was scared to death. In that instant, my first thought was that a big grizzly was staring at me. Many other thoughts rushed through my head.

As I gathered my thoughts, I calmed down. Finally I realized the eyes looking at me were those of my mounted trophy doe head. It had flown up in the crash from the seat next to me and landed right in front of my face. What a relief.

As I slowly got my bearings, I looked over my situation. Straight ahead of me, past the doe head, I could see straight down a deep cliff. Hundreds of feet down. Thank God for the huge tree that stopped my truck from falling to the bottom!

Now I was dealing with my body temperature. I was getting chilled. I had to get out and somehow climb up to the road to find help without falling off the cliff. And I had do it before the tree decided it didn't want to save my truck from the bottom.

I rolled down the window, pulled myself up with my

butt first and backed out of the window. I crawled up to the rear and slid down to the pathway the truck made as it fell, allowing me to make my way up the hill.

My fingertips and toes started to tingle. I knew then the temperature was taking over my body and that I had to keep moving. I thought I was well dressed until that point. I should have listened to the guys! Now what would happen to me? As I reached the road, I was freezing. I felt my face and teardrops had frozen to it. My eyes were watery and my Red Wing boots weren't warm at minus 50.

Keep moving. Keep moving.

All I was thinking was to keep moving. I started running down the road. My feet and boots were frozen solid as each step hit the ground. I wasn't really running, I was rather staggering, but I didn't stop. If I stopped, I knew I would die. I shoved my hands up my cuffs into my shirtsleeves. It didn't matter. The cold still managed to get its grip on me.

I had no hat, so the tops of my ears were stinging. I moved my hands out of my sleeves, one at a time, to cover them with my fingers, warmed them a little, then put them back in my sleeves. Icicles grew on my eyelashes. I ran and ran and ran.

Thank God! As I was running, I heard a motor. The sound of the engine grew louder. Finally the vehicle came into view. It was a truck and the driver immediately stopped, got out and grabbed me.

Realizing how cold I was, he rubbed me briskly up and down my arms and back as fast as he could as he helped me to the warm cab of the truck! It sure was good to feel the heat and to wrap myself in the army blankets he had with him. My hands were tender to the touch. It took both my hands and forcing my fingers to loosen the shoelaces on my boots. My hands and feet were burning from being frozen and I couldn't do much else for them.

We had to go a ways before he could turn around and go back to the nearest warm building on the road. I didn't care. I was safe and warm.

As we made a u-turn, we passed by the place I'd gone off the road. My rescuer let me know how very lucky I was and that I must have a guardian angel on my shoulder. The drop was so deep, had it not been for that tree, I would not have had a chance.

It wasn't far to a place called Lower Post, Mile 620 on the Alaska Highway. The driver was so helpful. He called the Royal Canadian Mounted Police on his CB as we made our way to safety. While we were driving, they were on their way to the scene.

By the time we arrived at Lower Post, I was still dealing with the pain of my body being so frozen, then rewarming, not to mention the shock of almost dying. There was a wrecker at Lower Post, so I sent it to pull out my truck. I wondered if my insurance company, much less Art, Paul or my mother, would believe any of this. I hardly believed it myself.

I got a booth in the restaurant and finally took off my boots, which was a very painful ordeal, only to find my toes beet red, even more so than my hands. I had to rub and rub them, trying to get my circulation back to normal while I had some hot coffee. As the truck driver was talking to the guys in the garage, explaining how to find the site and what he supposed happened, I was frantically trying to get feeling back in my limbs.

I was thawing out when I saw him coming back from the garage. I thanked him for saving my life and helping me out. When I offered to pay him something for all the trouble I caused him, he refused, but he had a cup of coffee with me. He was anxious to hear why I was out in the first place at -50 below and the rest of my story. We went through several cups of coffee when the Royal Canadian Mounted Police found us. I gave them all my information, a practice I was getting used to, and they told me I would be stuck here a day or two until the truck got pulled in and the damage evaluated.

This particular road stop was a rooming house rather than a motel or hotel. The rooms had cots and not much more. If there were better accommodations, I didn't see them. I didn't care, as the room was clean and, best of all, warm. I had to share the bathroom and shower down the hall. No TV anywhere. However, there was radio and a payphone in the entryway. Now that I was settled, the driver wished me luck, then went on his way.

Now I was alone and a new level of reality set in. I realized that all my new tires had blown out—just exploded from the rims. For the first time, I was really feeling shaken and frightened so badly I had to admit it to myself. I was SO scared.

The mechanics let me know that extremely high air pressure must have caused this to happen. I told them that when I had the tires changed in Saskatoon, I had 60 pounds of air put in. They both looked at each other in shock and let me know that this was the cause.

The passenger side of my truck was full of snow. When they pulled out the truck, snow filled the cab through the window I had crawled out of. Snow was caked in spots along the bed of the pick-up too. After everything was pulled out, they just let the snow melt in the garage. The passenger side fenders were pushed in, but other than that, just tires and minor repairs were required. The soft snow had saved me from a lot worse damage.

The camper shell had to be reset before the tie downs could be retightened. The mechanics had their garage full of cars and parts but still managed to make room for all my stuff, although not in a nice way. Maybe it was because of the narrow escape that I felt that way, but it wasn't like what the guys at Fort St. John at Jim's garage had done (which was to tuck my boxes neatly away).

I had no control over what happened in the garage. All the household items, clothes, artificial flowers and flower design supplies, my concertina, tires, and several cases of hunting gear were strewn around the garage for all to see. I had several cartons that contained Sorel hunting boots and catalytic heaters I purchased at a Kmart store in Wisconsin on sale. I had looked around at prices on things during my Alaska vacation and was sure I could sell them for double what I paid for them. I also had an antique National Cash Register I planned to make a profit on. All of these things I planned to use as a sort of grubstake while I got started in Alaska. At least I hadn't lost any of my nest eggs as far as my stuff went. And I had escaped with my life and didn't even have any broken bones.

Now I had to fess up and make my phone calls. The first was to Art. He couldn't believe I was in another wreck and still thinking about Alaska. The next was to Paul. I could tell by his voice that he didn't believe a word I said. Oh, well. He was the least of my worries. Then there was the call that I loathed the most. I called my mother.

Before the *"I told you so"* that I knew she would throw up at me, I cut the call short. I told everyone not to worry and that I was safe, not hurt, and would let them know when I would be leaving Lower Post. What I couldn't tell them was which direction I would be going or how close I had come to freezing to death.

Now that I had talked to the mechanics and made my phone calls to the insurance companies and family and friends, it was time to call it a day. After a late bite to eat, I went to my room. As I lay on my cot, the events of the day started gushing through my thoughts. I had pretty much thawed out by now, but I was very much aware of how close I come to freezing to death. As I lay there, my eyes were wide open and it took hours before I finally fell asleep. I wished I had a few drinks to calm down after all the excitement.

Morning came before I knew it and, even though I didn't get much sleep, I wanted a cup of coffee desperately. I got dressed, washed up, combed my hair and made my way to the café. As I was on my way to the café, I was still having flashes of what I had gone through. I think I was shaken up much more now than I was yesterday. It all became even more shocking and very real. I took the same booth as the previous day to have my coffee and a little breakfast.

I planned on checking on my truck after breakfast. I noticed three guys eating in the booth next to me. Eavesdropping, I learned that their vehicle, a Scout, had a heater problem. They were also delayed while it was being fixed. In these temperatures, they wouldn't get far otherwise. I sure knew that!

I wrote a few postcards, this time keeping in mind the right stamps needed, and called Jim to keep my friends in Fort St. John up on the latest.

I was so exhausted after that, I needed a nap. My body still needed more rest. I passed up lunch while I napped and felt the need to make more calls to Art and Paul. I knew Art had a map to keep track of my progress. I waited on those calls until I got the diagnosis from the mechanics and a timeframe as to when I'd be able to travel again.

During my wait for the news, I spent more time in the café. There was nothing else to do or that I felt like doing. Soon, the same three guys came in that were waiting on their broken down Scout. This vehicle was made by International Harvester to compete with the Jeep.

They were totally frustrated with their news. As I eavesdropped once again, I learned that the mechanics hadn't been able to fix their heater or get one to replace it. They were mulling around wondering what they were going to do. Their destination was Fairbanks. This was music to my ears!

I had a brainstorm and the method to go along with it, if I decided to do it. I could let them drive my truck in intervals of one hour at a time. We could rotate the guys between the two vehicles so that they could also drive their Scout to Alaska or a garage better equipped to deal with their problem.

I didn't talk to them right then and there because I

wanted to first talk to Art and Jim about how to handle it. In the meantime, I listened to more of their conversation and realized their intent was to trap and mine gold. It was the Alaskan dream for one of them. He looked to be the oldest of the three and wore a wedding ring. There was a very young man who was about 18 or so and seemed like he was just along for the adventure. At this point, after listening to him, I knew, if there was a way, he'd be gone. The third one seemed to be more of a partner in this venture.

The guys from the garage came in to give us the news. One mechanic for them and the other for me. I was told they could get the rims and tires and reset my camper shell, but I would have to get the bodywork done at another location better equipped. This was good news for me. I decided to go with everything taken care of except the dents. They didn't need to be fixed because they were only cosmetic damage, not structural. The news hadn't changed for the guys. We had exchanged a few hellos and a nod or two by now.

There were no telephone calling cards or 800 numbers in those days, just collect calls where the party you were calling paid for the call. Or there were hang-up calls in which the party you called would refuse to accept your call, but then called you back at the number you were calling from. Last, my least favorite, was dial-up and pay at the time of the call. Coin-operated payphones required lots of quarters anywhere in this country for direct calls.

Art would have liked to see me return. He was so sure that I would at some point. Women were so insecure and dependent on men where I came from.

I had to make a decision, one way or the other, whether to continue to Alaska or turn around and eat crow. I decided to go on. When I checked on the truck and went to get in, chills went up and down my back and the hair on my arms stood straight up. I just couldn't drive the truck. I was scared beyond description. I had to admit that my wings had been clipped.

As I thought more about it, driving in either direction didn't seem to make a difference. My gut reaction didn't change. My thoughts went back to the three guys, stalled here as well and still planning how to continue their trip to Fairbanks.

I walked into the café, gathering my thoughts and my bearings. Sure enough, the guys were having coffee, passing time while waiting for an update on their rig. I wanted to know a little more about them before I came to any kind of decision. I walked up to them, said hi, and asked how things were going. I sympathized with their situation, told them about my dilemma and introduced myself.

They were all from Marshall, Texas. The one with the wedding ring was Roger Rollins. He seemed to be the oldest and the decision maker of the three. The second oldest guy was Danny Langford, the cutest of the bunch, and the youngest one was Otis Keith Frances, nicknamed "Lucky," the gopher of the pack. He was always cold and wore a scarf even indoors.

The three seemed to compare their looks and have fun deciding who was the best looking. They also spent time dreaming what they were going to do with all the money they were going to make on the furs they would trap and gold they would mine.

The more I thought about driving, the more my thoughts of approaching them to drive seemed the answer. When I talked to Paul about it, he cut off the conversation. I am sure he didn't believe for a minute that I had another wreck causing another holdup. I know Art would have wired me any money I needed, as would Jim. However, there was no chance of that happening in Lower Post.

I finally built up enough nerve to try and work out a deal with these guys to get me to Fairbanks, so I approached them with the idea. They gave it some thought and said I could follow them until their heater was

138

repaired. It was some hope, not what I wanted, but I gave them some time to mull it over. The next day, the guys got more bad news. They would have to drive without a heater. This news made my truck look much more inviting.

I've never been one to take charity, so I made a deal. In exchange for getting me to Fairbanks, I would give each of them a pair of felt-lined Sorel boots, which was better than anything any of us had on, plus one catalytic heater. They, in turn, would get my truck started every day, check the oil, brush off the snow, and do any other maintenance that might pop up. It seemed like the thing to do and so we made a deal.

Triple Trouble from Texas

The next day when we decided to get on our way, ice fog filled the air as –50-degree temperatures set in again. The guys had a Ready Heater that they planned on using to get the rigs started each morning. There were few places along the way that were open. Most businesses were shut down for the winter and those that were open had limited plug-ins. Some had plug-ins available for a charge.

We all went into the garage to get the boots and heater out of my belongings to seal the deal. All my things were strung out all over the garage. The mechanics were just finishing refastening the shell cap and realigning it on the truck. It was almost ready to go. I would have to drive it with the fender pushed in and the damage to the front where it hit the tree.

A few days before, I thought it looked terrible. Sitting around waiting, healing my frozen feet and fingers, gave me time to think how lucky I was. My toes and fingers were healing now as they turned deep purple. They were stinging like the devil. Good thing I had a lot of lotion with me. My hands seemed to be very hard and sensitive to touch, even though a few days of babying myself had passed.

One thing for sure, the gear that I thought was the best had a lot of room for improvement. This morning, we all ate breakfast, looked over the maps, made some decisions where to gas up and what to expect. When we rotated vehicles, I didn't ride in their cold Scout. I had enough of being cold. We had a thermos and snacks in both rigs, plus extra gas and oil. I felt like I made a good deal that would take care of my driving problems. Soon my fate would be in their hands. I never let them know how much money I had or how scared I was to drive.

We took off after I made my collect calls, letting everyone know of my departure. I couldn't believe all the little ice crystals in the air and the exhaust fumes coming from their rig ahead of us. I knew we would have to rotate more often or the guys would freeze. I knew that we all had our long johns on. I sure was glad this little pick-up of mine had a great heater.

Fear of the weather was a concern, but I could see that the guys still underestimated how deadly it could be. Being from cold country and doing a little hunting let me think I was prepared. As for the guys, I think they just read about it. Winds started gusting, pushing my pick-up around. Since the camper shell was so high, it allowed the winds to put maximum force on my truck. We both had to slow down to keep in control of the vehicles. We were about 260 miles from Whitehorse, where we were heading, and about 300 miles from Fort Nelson, now far behind.

Our *Alaska Milepost* maps told us we would soon be entering the Yukon Territory and the next big settlement was Watson Lake. We would stop there and then somewhere between Watson Lake and Teslin. Rotating the guys seemed to be working out fine.

Cabins would cost about $30.00 a night for the four of us. We bought things for sandwiches, drinks and a deck of cards. We both had big dents in our budgets and so we had to watch the money we had left. Traffic had been pretty sparse until we got into Watson Lake.

I sure felt comfortable with the decision I made and had some interesting talks while learning about these guys. Roger was the son of a gas station owner, married with a family. Danny was single and going along for the

141

adventure, a cousin to Roger, and worked at the gas station. Lucky was also family, along for the ride and was 18 years old.

They had all kinds of questions for me. It seemed like they couldn't learn enough about me and couldn't believe I was traveling all by myself. They weren't traveling with much winter gear. They had a lot of tools, a few guns, traps, a Ready Heater and fuel. They were amazed at how much stuff I was hauling. They sure were interested to hear about my rifle.

The first day went pretty smooth and we decided to look for a place to overnight. We found a place that had cabins. They were dry. That meant that we had to haul wood and water. We had to start our own fire, heat water for washing and use an outhouse. Not too many choices. We all adjusted. We ate our sandwiches, made hot water for tea, played cards, and eventually went to bed. We all slept with our clothes on and agreed we'd get a place the next night with indoor plumbing even if it was going to be a little more expensive.

Now that I made a deal with the Texans to drive my truck to Fairbanks, we loaded all my belongings back into the camper shell. Swapping hunting boots and a catalytic heater for their skills and rotating drivers so they could warm up in my truck, let me relax a bit and leave the driving to them. Time to pull out the cameras.

I had about two dozen rolls of 110 film with me that I decided to start using. I took pictures of everything. I had an array of subjects. They varied from a herd of wild horses crossing the road and general scenery along the way to shots of the guys starting the rigs with a Ready Heater or target shooting.

They were pretty sure of themselves, zeroing-in on things with their rifles. They also had pistols to play with. They all thought they were expert aims and deadeye sportsmen. They had plenty of ammunition, enough to last quite awhile. They told me they got it at a really good price and that a lot of the bullets were refilled, what they called *reloading*. They actually took the empty shells and refilled them. They brought a machine with them that they used for this process. Every time the guys finished target practice, we all had to take a few minutes to gather all the used shells and give them to Lucky. He would reload them at night using his little machine, making them ready to use again. He also reloaded the shotgun shells.

I was now the cameraman and taking pictures for all of us. The daylight hours were shorter every day. There was talk about Alaska having total darkness in the winter months, but as yet, the daylight wasn't much different than I was used to in Milwaukee.

These Texans had a good sense of humor and goofed around all the time. They sure loved to pick on poor old Lucky. You sure could tell he was just a good ol' country boy. The other two were a little more streetwise. I was

Roger   Lucky

Roger and Lucky playing cards at night.

143

The guys using the Ready Heater to thaw their Scout. My truck is parked next to the cabin. Note how low it sets.

average streetwise in the city life, but realizing that, I was lost in this environment. If I hadn't made this decision to have these men drive me to Fairbanks, I would still be pondering what to do in Lower Post.

I labeled every roll of film with location, subject and date. I kept all of these rolls well documented so I could refer to them as needed. It was a good thing that I stocked up on film in Milwaukee, as it was about three times more expensive in Canada. It got even more expensive as things became more remote. I even took pictures of the guys shaving and pouring coffee from the thermos. Knowing I had tons of film, there was no limit to the pictures I took.

The men had cameras too, so they took some pictures as well. I kept everybody's film in separate bags and labeled them accordingly with each person's name. I also had a Polaroid camera. I didn't have a lot of film for this instant photo camera. This film was a bit more costly and about one third of the pictures per roll. I could get 10 photos per roll from the Polaroid and 36 photos per roll from the 110 film.

My truck was really loaded down and I'm sure it exceeded the half ton it was meant to handle. When the guys teased me about it, I just brushed it off. They laughed about all the artificial flowers I had. There were no silk flowers as we know them today. The classiest of the flower world in those days was velvet or flocked flowers. I had planned on making flower arrangements to sell during the holidays until I found a steady job.

I thought about Paul's offer to work for him, but remembering his tone of voice when I told him about my second wreck, I knew he thought I was pulling his leg and playing with his feelings. I could have cared less. At this point, my focus was on getting to Fairbanks. If stopping for target practice made my drivers happy, then that's what I'd do.

We took it slow and easy, but made steady progress driving only during the daylight hours. It was a wise decision given the sparse road traffic and dealing with these cold, cold temperatures. We didn't want to worry if we broke down in the dark. Animals were also a factor. They could jump out on the road at any moment and cause another wreck or even worse.

The guys sure were glad to have their new boots. These boots gave them a lot more warmth. They had thick felt liners that the boots they had been using lacked. I knew I could at least triple my profit on them. A customer would be very pleased with a price of about $79.95, a savings of about $25.00 for them, and a profit of about $50.00 for me. I was told I could make about $5,000 clear on my new truck when I bought it, if I wanted to sell it in Alaska. I knew that would not happen now, not with all the repairs and bodywork.

So far, we were only about half way to my destination and there was no telling what the future would bring on this trip. We would look for a place with indoor plumbing and hot water tonight. We found a place that charged us $50.00. That was cool with all of us. We all were looking forward to an evening of hot showers, hot water, indoor plumbing and, as a bonus, we even had a stove. We could cook and make coffee and hot chocolate. The guys were able to buy some beer. They all popped a top, got their reloading machine and powder out to fill their empty shells, and also played a few hands of cards. We all called it a night about 11 p.m., or so I thought.

I heard scuffing around outside throughout the night. I thought it was Lucky putting his reloading machine away. No worries.

Morning came early. Coffee was brewing when I awoke, and Danny had made bacon and eggs for all of us. We all took our time to shower and have breakfast while the Ready Heater was fired up. This large tube-shaped heater was about the size of a large vacuum cleaner. It was lit and set or aimed to throw a powerful surge of heat under the Scout. This bullet-shaped heater sure could throw the heat and the Scout started in no time. Then it was pulled over to my truck and after the same process, it started right up too.

Now all we had to worry about was checking the fluids and tires, brushing the snow off, gathering our gear, and setting up the thermos and sandwiches. Or so I thought.

Actually, there was a lot more to worry about, but I didn't know that—yet.

Alaska at Last

Another day's drive was ahead of us, and we were looking forward to making it to Whitehorse. We had left British Columbia and were now traveling through the Yukon Territory. Signs of civilization seemed slim—it looked more and more desolate as we went along. The day was pretty similar to yesterday. Even our routine was the same.

However, the scenery was awesome. Lots of taking breaks for pictures. We still were driving on gravel roads. Someone had told us that the roads were paved in Whitehorse. That was the good news. The bad news was that there was only 12 miles of it.

Whitehorse looked like a large town as we approached. There were about 11,000 people living there. (Fort St. John had 8,200. Lower Post had only a few hundred in the whole area.) There were lots of lights, buildings and businesses. Huge riverboats were drydocked on the shore. We drove around scouting the town to see what was open and what the town had to offer. Whitehorse was a very well kept town and clean. These folks had a lot of pride in the looks of their streets and buildings. Even if they were old, they were well maintained.

One thing we all noticed was an enormous billboard: Kentucky Fried Chicken. When we got closer, we all had a good laugh as the sign was bigger than the store. It was

KFC all right, about the size of a small bedroom, with only "to go" service. A bucket of chicken was dinner.

We rented a motel room and unloaded what we needed. Roger and Lucky wanted to walk around and see what they could see. Danny and I decided to relax. The bars were all open and seemed lively enough. My funds were very low, to say the least, and I just needed to save everything I could. I wanted to be sure I had money enough to get to Fairbanks.

About an hour and a half later, Roger and Lucky returned, telling about what there was for us to see. They called Danny outside for a little talk. I thought he was telling him where the girls or excitement was. Danny was a good-looking guy, and I'm sure he can find females wherever he goes.

I really didn't have much interest in him, but he was good enough to pass time with. Roger talked him into going out with them. That was fine with me. It gave me time to clean up, wash my hair, dry and curl it, and then take a bath that I totally enjoyed. I wrote a few cards while they were gone and played Solitaire.

The clubs or bars must have closed about midnight because the guys came in with a six-pack about then. They acted like they had enough to drink already. It sure is eye-opening to deal with people drinking when you aren't. However, they weren't too bad. Danny was a little suggestive though. There were only two beds in this room. We had to double up. Lucky and Roger in one, and Danny and me in the other. He, being kind of frisky, was not my cup of tea. He didn't push it, and I was glad.

As we all slept through the night, I heard noises and I realized the guys were outside and wondered what they were doing. They always seemed to have one of the guys inside, changing places, and going off somewhere. When I asked them what was going on, they said there was a party going on and they wanted to check it out. That seemed good enough for me. I knew something was up, but I didn't know what. Figured it was their business.

In the morning, we had breakfast in a cafe, did the routine check-up, gassed up and went on our way. Everything seemed fine to me. It wasn't long before we hit gravel road again. Oh well! We were all talking about getting closer to Fairbanks.

Our next stop was Haines Junction, still in the Yukon. This was a settlement and also a crossroads. There was a big roadhouse where we decided to stop, have lunch and get some news as to what to expect on the road ahead.

We continued on to Beaver Creek, just a few miles south of the Alaska Border. We took time to eat there, got our maps out and talked about our next stop. It was dark by now and our thoughts of pushing through all the way to Fairbanks faded.

When we hit the border, the agents there approached both rigs. We were in front at this point and the Scout was behind us. When asked if I had any firearms, I said, "Yes, a rifle." I didn't say anything about the pistol however. I didn't have a permit for it and didn't even mention it to the guys. I had it well hidden.

The agent asked to see my driver's license, birth certificate and title for the truck. I had to show a license and bill of sale for my rifle. As I scrambled for the paperwork they requested, the other agent was checking out all the paperwork and licenses from the guys. After he was satisfied with my paperwork, he asked to see my rifle, still in the box. As I reached behind the front seat and grabbed the rifle box, I realized it was empty. I am sure the surprise must have shown on my face. The agent asked if it could be anywhere else or in the other vehicle. I said no. After digging around, I asked the guys if they had seen it and they all said no.

The other vehicle and guns all checked out. Now I was being held to make a report. Never thinking it could be my guardian angel drivers, my thoughts went to the garage at Lower Post. I never even considered that anyone at Jim's garage could have taken it. All kinds of mixed thoughts flashed through my mind. The hold-up seemed to take forever. The forms were plenty. It's a good thing I had current paperwork with all the information they required. The guys wanted to get on the way, but the more I asked if we could go, the more information and forms the agents wanted.

Finally, they let us leave. I felt really bad. The rifle was like new, only used once. That was when I got my deer on a hunting trip. Nobody else had anything missing.

After we pulled out a ways, I asked Roger to stop the truck. I needed to get out. The northern lights were out in full glory and the stars were glistening like diamonds in the skies. I knelt down and looked up. I made myself two promises. The first was to **never punch a time clock again** and the other was to **never wear a watch again**. I was going to be a free spirit from this day on.

With that being said, we were on our way. We made it to Northway, just inside the Alaska border. It was apparent this was a Native settlement. The beadwork in their little store was outstanding. There were a number of crafts showing off the beadwork: slippers, purses, headbands, guitar straps, wristbands, earrings, medicine bags, etc.

We rented a cabin that night. Again, it was a dry cabin.

Billiard Queen of the North

Northway was a decision-making stop in the road. We were going to get to Fairbanks, about 250 miles, or split this leg of the trip and overnight somewhere near Delta Junction. We would easily make it to Tok, then Tanacross, then Delta, about halfway to Fairbanks. We decided to go as far as we could. The itch was in all of us. To get there meant a new beginning for all of us to pursue our dreams. Now it was early December. It seemed like I had been on the road forever.

We crossed the border December 5th, 1971.

Coincidently, this was Art's birthday. However, I had forgotten it. I was more excited about crossing the border. Things are becoming a reality now. I'm almost a pioneer, even if I fudged a little by getting help with the last half of the driving.

We decided to spend an hour or so in Tok gassing up, checking everything and getting a bite to eat. We made it to Delta and overnighted in another dry cabin. Funds would get me to Fairbanks with barely enough left over to get me to Healy, my final destination, or so I thought.

This day was to be our "Welcome to Fairbanks" Day. We were all excited because this is where we would part ways. The guys would go off trapping and gold mining and I would head on to Healy.

Fairbanks was bustling. Bars open all up and down Two Street, otherwise known as 2nd Avenue. I was dazed.

Other businesses open included Big Ray's Clothing Store, Co-op Drugs, the Bakery Restaurant, a number of other shops, even a barbershop owned by a black woman. This was the main part of the town. You could find anything you needed right here. If it wasn't here, you didn't need it.

Lots of pool tables and lots of guys meant lots of opportunities to win lots of money from unsuspecting pool players! All of these plans had to wait. We all ate supper at a place called Neta's Cafe. Lots of food, good prices and great service. A working man's restaurant. This was our last meal together.

As we left the café, I almost immediately noticed that my spare tire, which had been affixed to the rack under the bed of the pick-up, was missing. I didn't know how long it was gone or if it just happened. Nobody seemed to know. Now, I had to make my way to Healy without a spare. First my rifle and now my spare had disappeared.

We parked both of the vehicles in a parking lot next to Big Ray's. We were lucky to get a room at the Fairbanks Hotel. I guessed it had to be the oldest hotel in Fairbanks. It had old spring beds and shared bathrooms. The rate for all of us was $38.00. We thought we got a bargain, as we all needed to clean up.

We sorted our belongings. I had piled up 16 rolls of film in my bed and got them ready to take them to the Co-op Drugs for developing. I had stopped in there earlier to find out it would take about a week or ten days. When I gathered them up, Roger stopped me and talked me into letting him mail them to his wife along with his to be developed.

He assured me she could get them done cheaply, have copies made for them and mail the originals to me in Healy at Paul's. Because my funds were limited, I agreed. He also told me he would have her send me a copy of their prints as well. I went to the Co-op anyhow to make my calls to Art, Paul and my mother.

We got up the next day ready to go our separate ways.

I spent my spare time trying to get a second-hand spare tire that would fit. I found a used tire at a place called Kelly's, not far from Neta's Cafe. I had coffee there while waiting for them to track one down. This tire would cost me five bucks. What a deal. I wanted to take my time and check out Two Street, where the action was, to shoot some pool when I came back to town. My priority was Healy for now. My truck was ready to go and so was I. People warned me again about the moose jumping up on the road. This was my greatest concern. I finally departed shortly past noon.

By myself again, it took awhile before I felt comfortable driving. I remember things going fine and was attracted to lots of lights and a business about 35 miles south of Fairbanks. I pulled in and found out I had 30 miles more to go to Nenana, the next gas stop.

This place, called the Halfway Inn, was jumping. I enjoyed a few drinks that some of the guys bought me. They were just curious who, what, why and where I was headed. I found out that this was going to be common procedure from here on out, as there weren't many new single girls around, especially at this time of year, unless they were visiting someone.

It was uncommon to arrive at this time of year looking for work or a rental. Everyone was pretty well set for the winter by now. With 30 miles to go to Nenana, I departed the good company. This next stretch was very treacherous as there was a series of sharp corners and curves. I found myself struggling in parts of the highway, if you want to call it that. The winds would hit the side of the truck, making it hard to handle.

It seemed longer than it was, but I finally could see the lights of Nenana. As I made the turn off the road to go into town, I realized this was a very short main street. It was only about six blocks long. There was a gas station, however, right on Main Street. There were several little businesses, a lodge, grocery store, two cafes, two bars, a railroad depot, post office and a community center all visible off Main Street. I checked my money and I was down to two dollars. I can't remember when I was down to that size bankroll. This was not enough to get me to Healy. Maybe it was, but I couldn't be sure. I didn't want to take any chances at this end of the trip.

I took my two dollars into the Moocher's Bar. The other bar was the Corner Bar. The Moocher's had a better-looking bartender, young and handsome. The Corner had a guy with a handlebar mustache named Dooley. I scooted up to the bar at Moocher's and, before I knew it, the drink I ordered was paid for.

In every bar in Alaska, somewhere along the bar, a chain or a rope would be dangling from the ceiling. Then it continued a distance, stretched out through hooks or I-bolts, and attached to the house bell. If someone accidentally pulled the rope or chain and rang the bell, they would be obliged to buy the whole house a drink. This was the unwritten law. (This also happened when a customer was buying a round to celebrate an event, winning a bet or losing at a game of pool or darts, if that was the bet.)

There were several quarters lined up on the pool table. Lots of business for the Moochers. Everybody knew each other and it was a full house for sure. As I nursed my drink, the bell rang again. Another free drink. All right!! All this time I was watching the pool table and the guys shooting. They were shooting for money. Right up my alley.

I asked the bartender if anyone could play. He said sure, put your quarter up. That was good news, because I now had eight quarters for the two dollars I had. It was only about five in the afternoon, but dark, making it feel later. There were several quarters ahead of mine, so I had a little time to flirt with the guys. The bartender's name was Clifford Jury. He was pulling for me to kick butt when my time came. Finally, it was my turn. I was thinking, let the

154

games begin!

My strategy was "I came in here with two bucks and if I leave with two bucks, what the hell." I could see I was going to have fun here. I won the first game and from then on I had control of the table. My game was eight ball. Call every shot. I played just well enough to keep the table.

It wasn't long until Speck came out to relieve the bartender. He was working the night shift tonight and got an ear full from Cliff and the crowd that I was winning the pool games. The guys were pretty good, but I was good too, and in some cases better. Speck was the owner and started side bets. Soon there was money all over, piling up. My pockets were filling up. I still had the table and the competitors were getting tougher, but so were the bets.

The next thing I knew, Speck put on another bartender, Boy Monroe. He had a great sense of humor. During a short break, I got to meet several of the locals. Tony Jensen was one of the guys, as was Freddie Paul. He had sled dogs that he ran in races. Wesley Alexander, Nick Monroe, Teddy Suckling, Paul Starr, to mention few, were some of the locals. John Jerry was the town drunk and used the "F" word all the time.

I was dressed in my everyday dress for driving the highway, but things were getting pretty hot. It was warm enough for me to take off my heavy red shirt, leaving me with a black V-neck sweater and jeans to play in.

So far everybody was having a great time, as I was kicking butt little by little. I had now won about 10 or 12 consecutive games with tougher ones to come. Every once in awhile, one of the guys would be good enough to get down to shooting the eight-ball and he would have to call his shot. When that time came, I would lean over the pool table, look at him and say, "where are you going with that shot?" He would lose his train of thought while trying to sneak a peek and ultimately missed the shot.

This gesture worked for me every time. The crowd would then roar in laughter. I would then finish the game, win the bet and gather more fans. Speck would make more side bets and I would greet the next player.

This continued into the wee hours. I had now worked my way into playing my 21st game. The gentleman that was up next let me know that he was well aware what I was doing and that he knew how much money I had already won.

He said to me, "OK little girl, I got your number. I've been watching you all night. I'll bet you double or nothing for all the money you have in your pockets and I'll even throw in a tune-up on that wreck you have outside."

His name was Sterling True. This was the bet of the night and the largest amount of money at risk. Playing for $5 to $10 dollars a game, I had $160.00 so far. I called eight ball and the eight ball in the side as my game. With this bet, if I should make the eight ball in the side on the break, Sterling would have to pay *double* the bet.

With that understood, it was so quiet, you could hear a pin drop. By this time Mae, Speck's wife, had come out. This was a really exciting night for the locals. With all the side bets made, I leaned over and broke. *Crack!* Balls flew all over the table and the eight ball headed towards the side pocket. It slowed way down just as it got right to the edge of the pocket and then—gracefully dropped in!!

The bar went wild! I think the building lifted right off the ground with all the hollering. Drinks on the house from everybody! Nobody would let me pay for a drink.

Sterling paid up and let me know he would give me that tune-up whenever I wanted. It was party time at the Moochers, but I still had a ways to drive.

Speck was good enough to open and let me buy gas, and I continued down the road to Healy. Bars were open until 5 o'clock in the morning all along the highway.

I had about 70 miles more to go. On the way south to Healy, I passed the Missile Club about 17 miles south of Nenana, named for the Ballistic Missile Early Warning System station at Clear Air Force Base. About 25 miles south of Nenana was the turn-off to Clear/Anderson. Then came Clear Sky Lodge, about 33 miles south of Nenana.

The rest of the road had few businesses, but there were a lot of windy spots. I finally came to the Healy crossroads. With another 7 miles to go, I felt pretty happy that I was at the end of my trip. I pulled into Paul's Roadhouse and walked into the bar. It was very cold that night, but I had gotten used to tolerating the subzero temperatures. I didn't even put on my jacket. Nobody was in the bar. It was about 4:00 in the morning. Paul was behind the bar. As I got closer to the bar, I could see he didn't even recognize me. Either that or he didn't want to know me.

I said, "Hi, I finally made it." It hit him then who I was. I had my hair down in a single braid. There was no make-up or bee-hive hairdo. I guess I looked pretty tough. I was totally exhausted, had a couple of drinks with him, and asked where my room was. Right then I could see that the housing he promised me was intended to be with him. That wasn't going to happen.

I thought about my Canadian back in Fort St. John. What a gentleman. He'd never assumed or presumed, but always let me decide what I wanted. Unlike Paul, who finally gave me his room for the night and said we would talk things over tomorrow. He did let me know, however, that there was no job. When things strung out so long, he gave the job to someone else.

This roadhouse owner, with two airplanes, a full-time job besides the bar, and a retirement income, lived like a rat in a small cage. His room was cluttered, tiny and had a military twin bed. It got me through the night.

When I finally woke up, it was to coffee brewing and bacon cooking. When I went out, a big man named Bob Moser greeted me. Paul told him to give me anything I wanted. Bob was working until 4:00 p.m. It was about 11:00 a.m. when I got up.

There was no tub in this place, only showers. I had a

concern about that right off the bat. Bob said there were no tubs. I had cleaned up, fixed my hair the best I could, and eaten Bob's great breakfast when customers started coming in. There were a few locals that had been waiting for some time. Bars closed at 5:00 a.m. and were allowed to reopen at 6:00 a.m. Bob said it gave the owner time to count the money and swamp the floors. I guess this was supposed to be a joke, but that's the way it was.

I went out to the truck to see about getting out my Sorel boots to show the customers so they could think about buying some. As I fumbled around the cartons in the back of the truck, I realized all my cartons were empty! *Empty!* I was stunned, shocked and overwhelmed at what apparently had taken place. Almost everything I owned and had in the back of the truck had been stolen! Even my linens were gone—pillows, blankets, sheets. The only things left were my accordion, concertina, a very heavy brass cash register and a few artificial flowers. My suitcase with a few of my clothes was also left. Everything else was *gone*. I almost lost my breakfast right there.

Bob called the Alaska State Troopers and Paul at work. By the time I had given my report to the trooper, it was about time for Paul to come home anyway. Now I was really depressed. Here it was, almost the holidays, and I had nothing to bank on. Nothing to resell to make money. It took about two hours to give the trooper all the information, and I finally realized those Texans were the prime suspects. The trooper got on his CB and put out all the information for all the pawnshops and bars to watch out for them.

It was time to let the Grys's know that I finally made it. They came up to the bar to see me. After I told them my story, I could see they thought that I had exaggerated. I let them know what I had to deal with at Paul's and they thought I would have to find somewhere else to stay if I didn't like the situation. They made me no offer to stay with them, however.

I met a couple, Wayne and Maxine Harrelson, at Paul's. Their daughter had gotten married, leaving them with an empty room. I made a deal with them for "room and board" for $25.00 a week until I got a place to stay.

The Harrelson's also had one of the local Duyck boys, Robert, staying with them. His folks lived too far off the beaten path for him to attend the local high school while living at home.

Wayne worked for the Highway Department and Maxine was a homemaker. This took care of one of my biggest concerns. Paul hadn't even gotten home yet to hear this additional news.

The news that I had been shamefully blindsided and robbed spread like wildfire. CB's were the most used communication and everyone had one. Soon Paul's Roadhouse was filling up with customers hungry for the whole horrible story. The trooper had Paul's number to contact me with any further news or questions. I met many more people because of this incident and renewed some past acquaintances.

I spent the next few days making a serious effort to apply for a job at every possible place I could. Every few days, I would call the troopers or they would call me for an update. I also found out that I possibly had coverage on some of my lost items under my homeowner's policy. That was the good news, but it wouldn't replace the lost money I could have made by selling those items.

While in Healy, I learned that the priests, pastors and preachers traveled to their congregations on a regular basis, depending on the weather. I was invited to go snowmachining with the single, very handsome Baptist preacher, Wayne Brockman. As we flew up and down the slopes, me hanging on to him tightly, we hit a berm and flipped the machine. We both flew off.

I landed on my back in the soft snow. Wayne landed near me and leaned over and gently kissed me! I was sure the snow melted around me. Later, John and Louise asked me how I enjoyed the ride and my escort. I replied, "It's enough to make me want to change religion." Wow.

A couple weeks went by when we finally got a break in the case. John Grys was riding the rail, checking the tracks in a speeder car. This was a small enclosed self-powered railcar for short-distance inspections. John had checkpoints with a railroad guy based at each one responsible for a certain stretch of the track.

On this project, John stopped at a flag stop called Ferry. Percy Duyck was the railroader responsible for this section of the rail. During their talk about the report, John noticed Percy had on a new pair of Sorel boots. John asked Percy where he got them. He said three guys traded the boots with him for a ride out to an old trapper cabin about ten miles up the track.

Percy showed John the vehicle they parked there. Guess what kind of a vehicle it was? Yes, a Scout. What were the odds? These were my crooks! It was funny that John, who hadn't believed my story about being robbed, was the one who found out where the Texans had gone.

John came home to tell Louise the news, and it just so happened I was there for a visit. After calling the troopers, John took me there. When we arrived, the troopers were already there. We opened the Scout to verify that most of the stuff left in the rig belonged to me.

Percy took the troopers out to the cabin, and they closed in on the thieves. He told us later that when they got there, the three guys were huddled around a wood stove, freezing. My linens and clothing were stuffed between logs. The cabin had so many logs without insulation between them that cold air was coming through faster than the heat from the fire could warm things up. The troopers surrounded the cabin with rifles, ready to fire. Percy said that you never saw anyone so glad to get arrested as those three. Trapping in Alaska was not as easy as this trio thought it would be.

There is no jail in Healy, so the troopers housed the

160

Texans at a local motel. The State of Alaska served them three squares a day until the traveling magistrate could come to Healy and hear the case. In the meantime, all the contents of the vehicle and the cabin were brought in as evidence.

Remember, all the roads were gravel, the weather was often hitting –40-to –50°F. The magistrate had to either drive or fly to Cantwell. So, it was a few days before the magistrate, Eileen Kozevnikoff, came to nearby Cantwell where she would hear my case, along with some others.

The guys lied, of course, and told the court that I gave them all my personal belongings and the hunting gear. But the magistrate didn't believe them. What would Roger, Danny and Lucky want with my clothes? But it was their word against mine. There was no one else who had heard or observed what had happened. They were ordered to forfeit all the goods, to leave the state and each to pay a $50.00 fine.

Most of the new things had been sold or traded. My rifle was sold in Whitehorse. Thinking back, all that secret buzzing I heard through the night was the guys unscrewing the camper and then selling what they could. They would then reset the camper to look like nothing was bothered. This apparently went on all along the way. There was nothing I could do about it even though they later told me how they did it.

I tried to put it all behind me. I finally landed a part-time job with the school system, doing their reports for four of the nearby grade schools. They only had to have an enrollment of eight students to set up a school with one teacher.

I also made a few hundred dollars making flower arrangements for Christmas and New Years.

My insurance eventually came through with a settlement on some of the items lost or destroyed.

I had an artist paint me four Christmas cards. I mailed them out to my mother, older brother's family, my sister's

TELEGRAM
RCA Alaska Communications, Inc.
1971 DEC 23 AM 8 09

TEL NR
DIS?
CLERK & TIME

620A PST DEC 23 71 LB015 MB349

M MWA096 SO ALASKA 7 PD MILWAUKEE WIS 23 330A CST

JOANNE TREGILLIS   001195

BOX 33 HEALY ALASKA 99743

DOLLY I LOVE YOU MERRY CHRISTMAS LOVE

BOB.

*The only telegram I ever received from my
brother was the perfect present
for my first Christmas in Alaska.*

family and my little brother John. It was all I could afford.
That was one lonely Christmas until a telegram came. It
was from my older brother, Bob. It read as follows, "Dolly,
I love you. Merry Christmas. Love, Bob." It was sent to
Box 33, Healy, Alaska 99743.

I got the telegram December 23, 1971. After growing
up in a household where we seldom enjoyed a hug or a
kiss, this was the best present I can remember.

A New Beginning

With all my belongings stolen, I didn't have much in the way of clothes. One thing I noticed was that the wardrobe of the rural residents was "blah" and plain. There was no need for a fashionable dress or make-up. It was more important to be appropriately dressed, fed—and armed. Warm practical clothes, such as an insulated parka and footwear, were more important.

Nobody blinked an eye about the price of food, fruit and vegetables. All the pick-up trucks had a rifle rack in the cab. It was always hunting season for something.

One day I had a taste for some fresh fruit. The local gas station also served as a small quick-stop and had a few choices. Off to the side of the cash register was a bowl of fruit that included oranges, apples and bananas, priced at one dollar each. Your choice, one dollar. What a deal. They would have cost a dime a piece back in Milwaukee. Take it or leave it! I had the best banana I ever tasted in months, and it cost only a dollar. To me, you can't put a price on some things. My craving was satisfied.

I remember stories of people coming for a visit and bringing things like fresh eggs and tomatoes that they hand-carried on the plane because it was almost impossible to get fresh things at a reasonable price in the rural areas.

A pig farmer named Don McKee traveled through the valley once a month with his pork chops, ribs, sausage and roasts—cut, labeled and wrapped. The families were all glad to see him. Since almost everyone was living on a subsistence diet of wild game, fish and berries, domestic meat was a treat. People didn't run to Fairbanks, about 125 miles one way on gravel roads, to shop at a big supermarket.

December had very little daylight. This could be very depressing for many reasons. There is a term called "cabin fever" used all the time in the colder months. The darkness was the most common thing that would drive one to cabin fever. This was nothing to take lightly. It was a very serious mental stress condition. The 20th of December is the darkest day in Alaska, with almost 24 hours of darkness or twilight in many places.

Another reason cabin fever strikes folks is the lack of communication products. In certain areas, and this area was one of them, there was no reception for radios or TV. There was only one educational TV station (PBS) and a radio station. Telephones were limited in the area, so it was very costly to make long distance calls. Also, roadways and windy canyons kept planes from flying in and out.

A lot of women couldn't handle this lifestyle. New women were often called "imports" and you never knew if they would make it through their first winter.

Looking for a job was a daunting task. I daily visited every possible place that might need an employee. This included Usibelli Coal Mine, Golden Valley Electric Association, the Alaska Railroad, the school district, the Alaska Highway Department, various roadhouses, and all the other local businesses. Driving a school bus was my last choice, but I would do it even with my limited driving experience.

I became a regular woodtick (pest). Then, after the holidays, I got a break. I was to interview for a job as an office helper at the school. This part-time job was for a traveling secretary to five schools in the rural areas working one partial day a week per school. There were other applicants for the job. These were locals that didn't need a job and had shakey track records. Most of them were housewives with their kids in school. There was one single girl who was a college graduate and the daughter of two of the local schoolteachers. Her name was Jessie James. During the interview process, she accepted another job at Otto Lake, one of the local bars. That left the slot open for me. I got the job. I was very good at doing the books and reports. The school district put the emphasis on that.

I would drive to Cantwell, about 80 miles round trip, on a very treacherous gravel road. The highway followed the Nenana River canyon, known as "glitter gulch," for about 5 miles. There were several drop-offs with very few guardrails. Sometimes there were rock falls from the hillsides that would block the roadway for hours. Everything was very primitive in this area. There was no radio or CB reception. Travelers who turned back would have to find help or possibly attract a plane flying over. Sometimes it took hours to clear the rock falls.

One day a week, I would travel to Suntrana. This was in the heart of coal country about 15 miles from the Healy school. This school was located at the top of a single lane road that was very, very steep and crudely constructed. It was punched into the hillside of an area owned by Usibelli Coal Mines. This was a very small, one-room school with one teacher for grades 1-6 with eight-to 10 students. The teacher lived nearby.

Traveling the rough roads in this area was very dangerous. There was never a time I could make it up that hill to the school. I would just tremble when I looked at the drop-offs along that road. My flashback memories of my last wreck at Lower Post chilled me to the bone and the hair on my arms stood straight up. I would either leave my truck at the foot of the steep hill or the maintenance man would take over and drive it the rest of the way. His name was Dick Stickle. Dick was the maintenance man for several buildings owned by the school district.

One day a week I worked in Healy at the largest of all the schools with more than a hundred students. It had K-12 grades. High school students in the valley were all bussed to Healy, except for those in the Anderson Village School.

I was just a helper at this school. There was only a few office staff here. Claire Mercer was the senior staff person and we all followed her directions. There were many jobs lined up for each of us. Today, computers have replaced many of these jobs. The Healy Tri-Valley School was constructed with ATCO Units (metal trailers hooked together end-to-end or back-to-back to accommodate whatever was needed for the appropriate classroom.

This school had a very nice gymnasium that was used by all the grades. It also doubled as a community event center. I played music for some of the dances. It was nice to see the couples doing the schottische and ballroom dances.

The Anderson homestead did not have a functioning toilet or shower, but it served as my first home.

One of the best couples on the floor was Berle and Claire Mercer. She was my director and her husband was a local farmer/rancher who raised buffalo and mules and led guided horseback trips in the area. Hunters and people the government hired to do surveys and wildlife studies would contract Berle to guide them during their stay.

There wasn't a day I traveled the road that I didn't see an array of animals. It was quite overwhelming at times when caribou herds would cross in front of me as well as fox, wolves, coyote, moose, Dall's sheep, lynx, grizzly bear, porcupine, hundreds of hare, and lots of smaller animals and birds. It was always beautiful to watch the wild and free, not to mention refreshing. I was lucky to see someone walking a dog in the city.

One day a week, I would have to go to Brown's Court, about 30 miles north of Healy. It was another one-room school for grades 1-6. Older students were carpooled to Anderson for 7th and 8th grades or to Healy by bus. The parents could choose the option they liked best. This school had 8-10 students. One teacher lived on-site in an apartment attached to the school. Dick Stickle was also the maintenance man for this building as well. I spent a half-day a week here.

Finally, two days a week, I would travel to Anderson Village School to help out with the office duties. Bob Murray was the principal and soon became my permanent boss. His office was in shambles when I got there. There were piles and piles of files all over the floor of one of the rooms. Bob had no secretary.

When I reported back what I had to deal with, the school district decided to open up a secretary position at this school. I immediately applied for the job. I interviewed with Bob for the job. He was already aware how organized I was. During the interview however, I had to let Bob know one of my biggest drawbacks. I didn't know how to type very well! He already knew I was very good in all the other duties of the job. Even though Jesse James applied for this job as well, Bob hired me.

Finally, I landed a temporary, but good, job that would give me three-plus days work in one school, and a full week total in the valley schools. When Bob and I discussed my job, he noticed how unsure I was about typing. He made me promise that I would learn how to type better, and he would do the typing necessary for me after school. I would do everything else to the best of my ability.

I found it amazing that he would hire me. When we sat down and discussed it, he finally fessed up why he hired me over other qualified applicants of the area. He confessed that he hired me because I didn't know anyone and that he didn't want anything that went on at the school to be the subject of housewife gossip. There was no fear of that as my circle of people had very few housewives in it, let alone women. That was a deal I could keep.

While I looked for local housing in Anderson, I took a part-time job bartending at the Dew Drop Inn, right across the street from the school. I didn't know how to bartend either, or how hard it could be. Because there were few women in the area, all the bars and roadhouses would hire any woman they could find. The owners, Jean and Neil Witte, were from Minnesota so we had a lot in common. Neil said he would teach me how to mix drinks. When the time came, it was a very short lesson. He simply told me to fill the glass with ice and pour as I counted one, two, three, and add the mix. There were no blended drinks, so no worries there. I was great with this set-up.

During the weekdays, I worked in Anderson. I finished at the school at 5:00 p.m. and walked across the street to the Dew Drop Inn to finish out the night. If I worked on Friday, Bob would send his wife to Fairbanks for groceries and supplies. This was an all-day trip. She never got back home until after nine at night. That was OK with Bob.

About a half hour into my shift at the bar, here would be Bob coming through the door with his banjo. Let the

Bob playing his banjo at the Dew Drop Inn.
That's me on the accordion.

fun begin—me with my squeezebox and Bob on the banjo! Jeannette would stay behind the bar serving drinks while we knocked out some good ol' beer-drinking music. I know that Jean knew very little about those nights.

Neil didn't know I still didn't have a place to stay in Anderson the first night I worked for them and that I was spending the night at their place. Jeannette was going to Fairbanks the next morning. I awoke to some pans clanging on the stove and the smell of coffee and frying bacon. When I walked out to see what was causing the commotion, it was Neil making himself breakfast in his t-shirt and boxer shorts. Was he ever shocked when I walked up behind him and asked if there was enough for me.

I have to say he looked just as good with his pants on. We enjoyed a nice breakfast after I quit laughing. This job was the beginning of a lifelong friendship.

Jeannette introduced me to Dick McCready. He had a little house (some called it a shack) across the street from the bar. It was vacant and needed a LOT of work. It was small, with just room for a military twin bed in the bedroom. It had no hot water, as the tank had a hole in the side where rust had caused a leak. There was no toilet because the house was not winterized. The toilet had broken when the house was not heated while empty. There was a shower stall that Dick salvaged from a building that had burned. It was black from the fire. The same freeze that caused the toilet to break, also broke the pipes.

I really needed a place to stay if I was to work in Anderson. In winter, all housing was either occupied or shut down and winterized until spring. This little abode rented as-is for $100.00 a month plus utilities. I talked Dick into renting it to me with no money down, against his wife's wishes, and a promise to install a toilet. It didn't take long to figure out that could be awhile.

To my surprise about a week after I moved in, I came home from a long night at the Dew Drop to find a bucket with a toilet seat on top to hold me over until he could get the toilet installed. I bathed and ate at the Witte's until things were taken care of. You just adjust.

The positive side of the story was that I didn't have to drive the long road to Healy and I could party with my little clan of single guys at the bar. That was a tough job.

All the guys I liked were big money workers at the Clear Air Force Base. They were all civilians with good jobs and paychecks burning a hole in their pockets. I helped them out big time. If it wasn't the booze I poured for them, it was a game of pool they lost to me and the tips I made for cranking out their favorite song. This was the beginning of a new lifestyle for me. So far, I hadn't spent any time learning how to type!

Epilogue

So, now you know how I got to Alaska and what it was like living here before the big oil boom really put Alaska on the map. It didn't take long to acquire a following. Neal and Jeanette were pleased to stand by and let things flow—I made money for all of us.

I was attracted to a few of the local charmers. Ken Fulford, Chuck Weiler, Harry Pettis and Cliff Jury. Then there was this fellow, Monty Hawkins—tall, blonde, blue-eyed, physical, single and a confirmed bachelor. His days were numbered.

Those early days of gravel roads, poor communications and isolated communities are pretty much over, but if you know where to look, there are still some little out-of-the-way places here and there that can give you a feel of how it was in the early days.

More than 40 years later, I'm still here and have no intention of moving back Outside. I've been pretty busy enjoying "The Great Land." I don't want to call it work, but I've run a trading post, a restaurant—the Two Choice Cafe ("take it or leave it")—and what I call my "Bed and <u>Maybe</u> Breakfast." I was the first "Avon lady" in Alaska to deliver orders by dog sled and I've floated down the Yukon River on a barge trading merchandise to the Native villagers.

All these years, I've met more characters than you can imagine, and I've got lots more stories to tell. So if you like what you read, let me know and just *maybe* you can talk me into writing some more.

In the meantime, stop by and see me in Nenana. I've still got my gift shop. If I'm not there you just might find me playing my accordion on a tour bus while showing the tourists around town.

I bought this old cook stove brand new from Sears.

Order Form
Alaska: The Land of Men and Money

_____

name

_____

street

_____

city / state

_____

country / postal code / zip code

_____

telephone or email

Credit card information (Visa or Mastercard)

_____   _____   _____   _____

_____ / _____   _____

expiration date   security code

Make checks payable to Tripod Gift Shop.

Please send me _____ copies of Alaska: The Land of Men and Money

Price: $19.95 each. Postage and Handling: Add $5 for sending the first copy. We will bill actual cost for more than one copy sent to the same address.

U. S. orders:

Specify _____ Priority Mail (1 week) or _____ Media Mail (2 to 5 weeks).

International orders will be sent via Air Post and billed for actual cost.

Tripod Gift Shop
PO Box 129
Nenana, AK 99760
email: tripodgs@nenana.net   website: www.nenanaalaska.net
phone: (907) 832-5272 / (907) 832-5556

Chicken Stewed

Wash and cut up chicken in small pieces.
Melt one stick of butter in a pan, then add the chicken.
Brown chicken. Add salt and pepper while stirring.

Also add 1 pinch each of cinnamon, allspice, cloves, garlic
salt, parsley flakes and basil. Add one small diced onion.

Blend and stir all ingredients. Gradually add up to 2 cups
of water. This will make a brown gravy.

One variation is to add a tablespoon of tomato paste or a
small can of tomatoes.

Making my deliveries as the Alaska Avon lady, 1974.